Praise for
THE OTHER

"*The Other* is a love letter to every woman of color who has sacrificed her authentic voice and talents for a false sense of safety. No longer do we have to be reactive to our work environment. It's time to rise up and go after what we deserve!"

—Minda Harts, author of *The Memo* and *Right Within*

"A powerful, compelling read. In these pages, Daniela is the guide and mentor that many women look for and need when facing challenges at work. She mobilizes women to embrace their power, negotiate for more, and possess their own space, not just to succeed but to be successful. I could not be prouder of her journey and achievements."

—Mika Brzezinski, cohost of *Morning Joe* and
New York Times bestselling author

"If I'd had this book earlier in my career, I probably would have spent less time crying alone in the office bathroom. Essential advice from someone who has navigated these traps and hurdles with agility and grace."

—Alicia Menendez, author of *The Likeability Trap*

"*The Other* is an honest account of what it's like to feel marginalized in a traditional American workplace. Pierre-Bravo's story of rising the ranks in her career is engaging, useful, and—perhaps best of all—validating. Its underlying message of community and support left me feeling hopeful about the future of work."

—Kristin Wong, author of *Get Money*

"Reading *The Other* by Daniela Pierre-Bravo was like turning the camera on and watching my own life experiences be reflected back at me. A poignant manifesto on how to close the door on impostor syndrome and advocate for yourself and your successes. At times harrowing, but hopeful, *The Other* is a book that should be gifted to anyone who wants to work in a corporate space and should be required reading for people managers, especially those who manage BIPOC people." —Saraciea J. Fennell, editor of *Wild Tongues Can't Be Tamed*

"I could not put this book down! Daniela Pierre-Bravo has written an energizing, eye-opening manifesto for women of color to own our power, urging us to recognize how our hurdles can be channeled to become our superpower. Pierre-Bravo's story of her incredible rise from an undocumented immigrant to one of the most recognizable faces on television is riveting. Even more so, how this book creates a playbook and community for everyone who has felt like the 'other' to embrace, not shun, what sets us apart. Read it again and buy copies for all the aspiring leaders in your life!" —Ruchika Tulshyan, author of *Inclusion on Purpose*

THE
OTHER

THE OTHER

How to Own Your
Power at Work
as a Woman of Color

DANIELA
PIERRE-BRAVO

LEGACY
LIT

NEW YORK   BOSTON

Copyright © 2022 by Daniela Pierre-Bravo
Cover design by Tree Abraham. Lettering by Alicia Tatone.
Cover copyright © 2022 by Hachette Book Group, Inc.

Legacy Lit, an imprint of Grand Central Publishing
Hachette Book Group
1290 Avenue of the Americas
New York, NY 10104
LegacyLitBooks.com
Twitter.com/LegacyLitBooks
Instagram.com/LegacyLitBooks

First Trade Edition: August 2023
Originally published in hardcover and ebook by Grand Central Publishing
in August 2022.

Grand Central Publishing is a division of Hachette Book Group, Inc.

The Grand Central Publishing and Legacy Lit name and logo is a trademark of
the Hachette Book Group.

The Hachette Speakers Bureau provides a wide range of authors for speaking
events. To find out more, go to hachettespeakersbureau.com or email
hachettespeakers@hbgusa.com.

The publisher is not responsible for websites (or their content) that are not owned
by the publisher.

Grand Central Publishing books may be purchased in bulk for business, educational,
or promotional use. For information, please contact your local bookseller or the
Hachette Book Group Special Markets Department at special.markets@hbgusa.com.

Library of Congress Cataloging-in-Publication Data
Names: Pierre-Bravo, Daniela, author.
Title: The other : how to own your power at work as a woman of color /
Daniela Pierre-Bravo.
Description: First edition. | New York : Legacy Lit, 2022. |
Identifiers: LCCN 2022004458 | ISBN 9780306925443 (hardcover) |
ISBN 9780306925450 (ebook)
Subjects: LCSH: Minority women—Employment—United States. |
Minority women in the professions—United States. | Minority women—United
States—Psychology. | Businesswomen—Job satisfaction—United States.
Classification: LCC HD6057.5.U5 P55 2022 |
DDC 331.4/08900973—dc23/eng/20220504
LC record available at https://lccn.loc.gov/2022004458

ISBNS: 9780306925467 (trade pbk.), 9780306925450 (ebook)

Printed in the United States of America

LSC-C

Printing 1, 2023

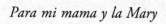

Para mi mama y la Mary

Contents

Introduction   xiii

1: Turn Off Survival Mode   1

2: Why You Feel This Way   15

3: When the Other Was Born   31

4: Take the Damn Risk   57

5: Duality Is Your Superpower   81

6: You Are Worthy   109

7: The Burnout   139

8: Repeat After Me: "My *Why* Is My Power"   151

9: Grab a Seat and Order Coffee Too   177

10: Go for More!   197

11: Your Career Needs a Manager   211

12: The Power of the Other   227

Acknowledgments   235

Introduction

I have to be honest with you: I had a hard time with the title of this book. The idea of being "the other" alludes to being different. At work it can feel like you stick out and don't fit in, which can be alienating and disempowering. But for the same reason you probably decided to pick up this book, I chose to keep the title. I've both felt like "the other" and been identified as one, whether consciously or not, due to being an undocumented, first-generation-immigrant Latina. Being othered suggests that you don't belong. You don't fit in. It's a duality that many women of color, immigrants, and children of immigrants have to navigate our entire lives. And many of us have spent a long time and lots of unnecessary energy going along with implicit rules about identity to fit into a white world, hiding our differences in order to be accepted in both our personal lives and our careers. These rules are tied to the differences in our cultures, races, ethnicities, socioeconomic backgrounds, and so on, and they suggest that achieving conventional success would be easier if we hid, repressed, and shielded parts of ourselves so that we could "belong."

This feeling of not belonging is magnified when we enter a workforce where many of the other employees and higher-ups don't look like us. While representation of women has improved in the overall corporate landscape, a McKinsey "Women in the Workplace" 2021 study highlights that women of color navigating their careers from entry level to the C-suite drop off by more than 75 percent and account for only 4 percent of C-suite leaders. It's no wonder many of us feel the gaps our duality creates between us and the people around us on a daily basis. We feel forced to shape-shift and conform at work to try to achieve success, because we've worked our butts off to get there. And I've written this book to help you develop the right mindset and know-how to come to work with the fullness of who you are and get what you deserve.

I was born in Chile and permanently migrated to the United States with my parents at age eleven. I grew up in the shadows in a small town surrounded by messages that said people like me did not belong. As an immigrant and the oldest of five siblings, with parents who struggled despite working two to three jobs each, I saw assimilation and blending in as my best shot of achieving the bright and shiny American Dream. The rules I created for myself in order to be included took on different forms throughout my life and followed me into the workplace. And my strategy proved successful. I'm an on-air reporter for MSNBC's *Morning Joe*; I coauthored my first book, *Earn It!*, with Mika Brzezinski; I'm a TEDx speaker; and I founded a mentorship program called Acceso Community. But it wasn't easy to create a new narrative for myself as an "other" to get there.

I also realize that as a Latina who is fair-skinned, I didn't fight half the battles many other women of color have had to reckon with, such as the systemic issues that disproportionately continue to affect them in the workplace. That's why, as I share my journey here, I've also made a point to acknowledge and recognize the perspectives and experiences of Black and brown women who have to deal with the deep-seated layers of microaggressions and outright prejudice that still prevail in our society today.

This book will show you how I built the confidence and broke through challenges to stop letting other people dictate how far I could take my career. It's about how I took back my story and flipped the script.

It was my very feeling of otherness that made me want to reach for success even more. But that feeling also limited me. The truth is, as women of color, immigrants, and children of immigrants, we have a different experience when climbing the ladder toward success. I realize now that there are many challenges and assumptions that get in the way of us taking up more space at work, using our voice effectively, and achieving our career goals. That's why I wrote this book.

Learning to accept and step into the power of being different, finding ease and confidence in being who we are, is the very thing that ultimately will make being different your competitive advantage. It's not a setback, and you should no longer accept that narrative. Your uniqueness is a power that only you possess, and *The Other* is going to show you how to use it to get what you want at work and in your career. My hope is that, after you read this book, you move like a wildfire toward your goals, that you master using your unique voice effectively to get the raise, the promotion, the next-level job, or whatever other career goals you're set on. I want you to embrace your authenticity, cultivate an ease in being who you are, and believe you deserve your success.

Aside from putting in the effort to be excellent at what you do, working twice as hard for half the reward, I'll bet you've also had to expend energy to manage other people's perceptions of you, dealing with bias and microaggressions that turn into energy-sucking doubt, hesitancy, and a need to appease.

It's time for you to stop waiting for anyone's permission. It's time for you to play big unapologetically and use your multidimensionality to your favor. It's time to get what's yours—to be who you are fully, come out of the shadows, and take up space as you are.

This isn't going to be your typical career book. This is a book for us and about us.

The journey we'll take together through these pages will help you take power over your own narrative, break barriers at work, and relish your strengths and value—from a place so deep in you that nothing will make you question your place in any workplace or career. You are unstoppable. It's time to take a big piece of the pie.

THE
OTHER

1

Turn Off Survival Mode

Growing up, I knew that I had the chance to do something my immigrant parents never did: build a career that meant something more than living paycheck to paycheck. Discipline, scrappiness, and going a mile a minute were not only traits that helped push me through the current of chaos and instability—they also felt like they were part of who I needed to be to stay focused on the goals I was hungrily pursuing. My ambition meant never taking my foot off the gas pedal. It felt counterintuitive to slow down, as if doing so would mean I was lazy, careless, or maybe even reckless. I was in the land of opportunity, and I wasn't going to do anything to derail what was possible ahead.

If hustle culture were its own city, I'd be the mayor. But, as you'll read, I eventually hit a plateau in my career. Years of valuing productivity as a way to prove myself led me to equate my value with how I showed up for others. But at a certain point, staying in that gofer mode was getting in the way of my professional progress. In order to climb up the ladder, I needed to do more. Yet when it came time to express my ideas and advocate for them, I found myself holding back.

When you come from a place where you learn to survive by living through the expectations of others, it affects your ability to excel and find ease in being yourself. Instead of focusing on self-development and seeking new and better opportunities, you get stuck on "getting it right." As if there's a gatekeeper between you and your success whom you've got to keep happy.

Many women of color and children of immigrants may understand when I say that I grew up in survival mode. It meant my family was constantly running from one thing to the next, doing our best to get through the next twenty-four hours, the next week. We couldn't plan too far ahead because we hardly knew how to make it to the upcoming month as we tried to survive financially, manage our never-ending housing insecurity, and deal with the chaos of being uprooted.

I'd like to tell you my parents did well for themselves with this chance at the American Dream. That their hard work, endless jobs, and long hours gave us a comfortable living in our new life in Lima, Ohio. But the truth is that we struggled and would continue to struggle for a long time. I watched as my parents opened unsuccessful restaurant after unsuccessful restaurant, right around the time our small community was hit hard by the 2008 recession. Lima is a town of less than 40,000 people in northwest Ohio, about two hours away from any major city. Like any other industrial town dominated by steel, manufacturing, and the local oil refinery, it has borne the brunt of economic booms and busts. The many empty warehouses serve as evidence of the factories that have come and gone.

Shortly after we moved to Ohio from Chile, my father, who worked as a line operator at the health technology company Siemens and was eagerly making plans to obtain certifications to help him land a promotion, was laid off unexpectedly as the plant announced its closing. Our family scrambled for a plan B.

The tricky thing about being new immigrants to a small city with no networks or professional contacts was that each time my parents were laid off or one of their entrepreneurship aspirations failed, they had to start over from scratch. They worked hard for what they earned, and their priority was always putting their kids' education first at all costs, but honestly, they were never good at managing their money properly. As a result, bills accumulated and savings remained low, which would affect my siblings and me down the road. Tension and screaming matches brought about by stress from all sides were the toxic status quo in our home, triggered by the volleyball games I had to miss because we didn't have gas money, not being able to do homework because the internet bill didn't get paid, and so on. I've never quite forgiven myself for all the outbursts and pressure that I placed on my already-overworked mother, who day after day placed her own physical health at risk working jobs that called for physical labor because they were the only jobs she could find. My reactions stemmed from the pressure I was putting on myself to belong and to excel. It was a factor I couldn't control, but it also had a major role in shaping my extra-meticulous, judicious, organized, responsible, and very much type A personality.

Admittedly, my relationship with my family is complicated. I would gamble and say you would agree that no family is perfect. But above all, my parents gave us something great: a chance to be in a country where we could make our own decisions, choose our own destinies, and seek out our own dreams.

Their emphasis on our education meant that by the time I hit high school, they managed to send me to a private Catholic school that we could barely afford. My mother would have recurring conversations with a school financial administrator, who warned her that if we didn't make our payments, I would be pulled out of class. This went on for four long years, during which I dealt with the stress of not knowing if I'd still be in the same school the next day, while my mom had to deal with the humiliation of the financial administrator chastising her.

"Your daughter will grow up to be no one in life with this sort of example," she said, referring to the "irresponsibility" of my family's late payments. But my mother ignored her harsh remarks and remained steadfast, pleading for an extra day, promising the next payment would come ASAP. And it would—very slowly, while my mom endured the reprimands of this stranger who said things like, "Your daughter should be out working for her education." The financial administrator probably thought she was teaching us an important lesson, but if she could've spent one day in my mother's shoes, she would have understood how out of touch her assumptions and unsolicited advice were.

"I wish I would have done a better job defending myself," says my mother now when we recall those meetings. But as a newcomer with only broken English to get by, she didn't yet have the confidence to stand her ground. Speaking to other first-generation immigrants, I know this is a feeling that arises all too often. Her focus was on keeping me in school, even if it meant swallowing her pride and dealing with the anxiety of it all. And it worked. That high school provided access to opportunities like AP classes and plenty of extra-curriculars to choose from, and I threw myself headfirst into every single one within my reach. This meant that I signed up for musicals even if I only got background roles, and despite being incredibly unathletic, I enrolled in sports throughout the school year.

The feeling of always needing to do more and do it faster to compensate for our situation stuck with me, as did the constant angst that at any given moment, we could lose everything—because many times we nearly did. I normalized the scramble. The anxiety. The constant surge of adrenaline. And then my toxic addiction to it: If there was no angst, then I unconsciously felt I might be doing something wrong, because most of my family's wins happened when we were teetering on the brink of falling apart. Because nothing in life was certain and there was always so much at stake in even the smallest of opportunities.

Like the time I felt my life had been struck by a 9.5-magnitude earthquake that threatened to demolish my one shot at developing my professional life and education.

It was a hot late afternoon in mid-July, the summer after my freshman year of college, and, as on any other weekday, I was out on delivery runs for my Mary Kay beauty and skin-care consulting business. With my windows rolled down, I breathed in the scent of Lima's freshly mowed suburban lawns while doing a quick mental check of the best route to drop off bags of products and reach my consultation with my new client Renee on time. That's when the phone rang, snapping me out of the map I had laid out in my mind. It was one of my repeat customers, Angela.

Against my better judgment, I flipped open my Razr cell phone and brought it to my ear. (This was pre-headphone days, and if I'd put Angela on speaker, the noise streaming through my open window would've drowned out my voice.) With one hand on the wheel and the other holding my cell, I almost missed my turn as I struggled to pay attention to the voice on the other end.

"I can't for the life of me find the color from last time," Angela said, "and I wondered if you knew...Hold on, I think I—"

Bam! I jolted in my seat, my body secured in place by my seat belt, my heart jumping into my throat, as my car came to a crashing stop. Blood rushed to my face. I frantically glanced around to get my bearings. When my eyes met the windshield, I realized there was an old, run-down beige minivan parked in front of me that I had just fender-bended. *How. Did. This. Happen?!*

"Found it! Apple Berry!" said Angela in her cheerful voice, defibrillating me back to reality. "That was the lipstick shade!"

"O-o-okay," I managed to whisper back, trying to conceal my heavy, panicked breaths. "I...I have to go now. I'll...I'll be delivering it shortly," I promised. Desperate to hide the fact that I had just hit a parked car, I added, my voice wobbly, "Thank you again for the order!"

Light-headed, I ended the call, my cell phone sliding out of my hand and onto my lap. The deep pit in my stomach felt like it was sucking the blood supply from every inch of my body. A stream of nightmare scenarios flashed across my mind: Jail. Never going back to school. Separated from my family. Detention center. Deported. I squeezed the steering wheel until my knuckles turned bright white.

It was the end of a series of eternally long workdays, and I had been pushing through a wiped-out feeling that was quietly taking hold of my body and mind. I shouldn't have been driving that day. I didn't know it then, but I was swimming in my own survival mode, yet I couldn't and wouldn't stop until I reached my goals. I was slated to return to Ohio's Miami University for my sophomore year in just a few weeks, and everything was riding on how much money I could milk out of these last few weeks of working my numerous side gigs, including my work at Mary Kay. Since I was unable to apply for government scholarships or loans due to my undocumented status, and my family didn't have the means to pay for my college education, I had to find creative ways to afford each semester's dues. Aside from a small private scholarship that I received and some college credits that would transfer over from my AP classes, I knew there was really only one possible way to get to the finish line: pay it all in cash.

Jobs like restaurant work, babysitting, and Mary Kay consulting, which others may have seen as minor side jobs, took on new meaning and became serious opportunities for me. I was first introduced to Mary Kay by a friend who mentioned a lady at the mall complimenting her skin and offering a "free makeover." What started as a fun opportunity to get one-on-one makeup advice turned into a life-changing opportunity: a vital piece of the financial puzzle that would help me get through college. The piling on of all those side gigs had already gotten me through my first year. Now my future was riding on doing everything in my power to save as much as I could that summer and get another round of semesters under my belt.

While some of my friends were unwinding from their school year poolside, my mornings began at the back of a Mexican restaurant, cutting limes and setting up for our nine a.m. opening. At around one p.m., I'd have an hour-long lunch break and then clock into the second shift. Depending on the day, I'd rotate between being a busser, a waitress, or a hostess. Luckily, I had the chance to train in all three roles, which made finding an available shift easier at any given day. After leaving the restaurant around five, I'd run home, trying my best to quickly scrub off the smell of fajitas before transitioning into a Mary Kay beauty consultant extraordinaire.

My late afternoons were spent offering makeup and skincare "parties" to strangers in hopes that I would at the very least make one sale. I found myself constantly looking for ways to up my game so customers would take me seriously. I'd offer a bonus follow-up service delivering the purchased products straight to the client's door. Repeat customers like Angela, who bought Apple Berry lipsticks and eye makeup remover every five months, were my priority. I could count on their fifty-dollar purchases (before tax), twenty-five of which was my take-home commission. Add up all the Angelas and their referrals, and my delivery service was worth it. Which is why I tried to squeeze it all in, to keep going and stay afloat. Every little bit I could do added up.

I was constantly racing against the clock and doing way too much at once in an attempt to manage the swirl of uncertainty ahead. I was exhausted and mentally overloaded, my mind on autopilot, always trying to think two or three steps ahead of everything. It's how I had conditioned myself to survive in my environment, a lesson I had incorporated into my life ever since my parents decided to leave Chile for good and follow the American Dream. A lesson that would appear over and over again throughout my life and career.

Only, on this particular day, my nonstop hustle had finally caught up with me. Maybe it was the fact that I was driving without a license or answering a client's call while driving, or the fact that I was semi-speeding in order to make the list of deliveries before dark. (I hated driving at night for fear of being pulled over and caught without documentation.) For a split second, I had lost control, and now the consequences could be devastating. My education was at stake. How could I have made such a rookie yet colossal mistake? Why did I miscalculate the sharpness of that left turn? All I had to do was drive down that street and park in front of the porch where I was due to leave the next Mary Kay delivery. Out of all possible scenarios, I couldn't believe hitting a parked minivan would be my undoing. A fender bender at that.

I walked over to the front of my car that day—well, really, the car I had borrowed from my parents—and immediately noticed a deep dent in its front bumper. My heart sank. I knew what I had to do, but what if this person called the cops? What if they found out I was undocumented? What if they took me away and I never got to see my family again? Paralyzed by an avalanche of fear, my only thought was: *I need my mom.* When I reached our house, I waited outside until she came home. The minute my mom stepped out of her car, I burst out with the story, struggling to find the words to explain what happened. She walked over to me, digesting my agitated state and the possible consequences of this turn of events, but instead of chastising me, her voice softened. "Una cosa a la vez," she said. One thing at a time.

In a normal situation, I would have exchanged insurance information with the car's owner and we would've gone our separate ways. Instead, I offered to pay her cash to avoid getting the police or any third parties involved. Normal also would have meant having a driver's license at age twenty. Normal would have been simply enjoying my first summer break from college.

Normal would have been not having three or four jobs to save up enough cash for school because I didn't have access to any form of financial aid. We were far past normal in many ways.

There were no safety nets.

I had managed to stash away a couple thousand dollars under my mattress that summer, and although it was nothing close to the full tuition for the year, those savings, coupled with the private scholarship and my plans to continue working cash-paying jobs, were enough to get me back on campus in the next few weeks and figure it out along the way. But that night, with my mom alongside me, I went back to the owner of the car and handed over my wad of hard-earned savings, suddenly feeling my future disappear before my eyes.

What now . . . what now . . . what now?

After I handed over the cash to the owner and left to go home, numbness washed over my body as my mom turned into the Ray's Supermarket parking lot in silence. My little sister had been sitting in the back seat all along, quietly witnessing my unraveling.

I glanced over at my mother. No matter the struggle or impossible situation ahead, my mom was always the one who forcefully told us that "todo tiene arreglo." Everything can be fixed. And I'd revisit that advice for years into my career. She always made us feel like we were on our way to something better. She was never without a can-do attitude, and always had a deluge of opinions and advice. But this time she had no words left to offer, underscoring the gravity of the situation.

Sitting in the passenger's seat, I watched her downcast demeanor, fighting painful knots in my stomach and tears that felt like they were drowning my every breath. After what felt like an eternity, she turned to me, full of empathy and sadness.

"It's not fair to you. You worked so hard." Her voice was barely audible through what sounded like a lump forming in her throat. "It's not fair to you," she kept repeating as tears streamed down her face.

Before that, I had seen my mom cry only once, when I was seven years old. I was upstairs in my room flipping through books when I heard her devastated shrieks. She had just received a phone call announcing that her dad, Tata, my grandpa, had passed away suddenly. It took thirteen years and a miscalculated left turn to bring her guard down in front of me enough to openly share her tears again. In the parking lot, we wept together, quietly holding each other, trying to make sense of the moment. This time there was no "We'll take it step by step" or "We'll figure out a way around this." We had played all our cards.

I was exhausted. Defeated.

That night I paced back and forth in my room, then flung myself to the ground, my hands pounding against the floor. I screamed my anger and devastation into my pillow and then out loud, without caring who could hear. It was a cry for help, one I knew would be in vain. Reaching out to the rosary on my bedframe, I held it tight and curled myself into a ball, pleading for answers to get me out of this mess, until eventually my tears gave way to sleep.

After months of ramping up my work hours, working seven days a week, often fifteen-hour days, I managed to get back to school.

As you'll learn, I eventually started my own path in a new city, became financially independent, and gained access to work successes seemingly beyond my means. Survival mode took on a new form in my life. This survival mode followed me into the workplace as I did everything I could to stay afloat, clinging to every opportunity to break out of the box society had created for me as an undocumented Latina.

Survival mode marred my self-awareness. When you're constantly trying to subsist, there is no room to question the why behind your actions and progress. Survival mode wasn't just about my money or my goals; it was omnipresent in other ways in my life. Surviving in white American culture meant carrying the weight of inadequacy in every interaction I had and constantly feeling like I had to prove myself at every turn, whether the moment called for it or not. With every achievement, from getting my first job to starting at MSNBC and onward, I held on to the sense of having to prove that I belonged there. I learned to survive by hiding part of my identity, the fact that I was undocumented, the shame it made me feel. I swept it under the rug, pretended it wasn't there, and kept forging ahead to succeed for myself and my family. It's what I needed to do to create some sort of psychological safety for myself and keep going. But all that did was confirm to myself that I was an "other," without making space for anything but repressing my own guilt and self-judgment over it.

But as time went by and my career and work experience evolved, I realized that having a seat at the table and using it meant the level of my productivity wasn't enough, a counterintuitive notion to what I learned growing up. The *quality* of my work value, one that called for me to express more confidence and gravitas, was what I needed to tap into and show more of. Could it be that the very thing that defined my immigrant ethos was starting to work against me as I grew in my career? The immigrant and BIPOC (Black, Indigenous, People of Color) story—working hard, being humble, and navigating our careers with empathy—is one of the greatest generational gifts we have received, but as we move up in our careers, this narrative's effects on our work lives can be more complicated than they initially seem. I realized that I needed to reevaluate how I was showing up at work and figure out what I ultimately needed to do to achieve not just success but also happiness, peace of mind, ease, and assertiveness at work. To climb further up the ladder, break glass ceilings, and move into our greatest power, we have to start from within.

2

Why You Feel This Way

Why do I feel stuck? Am I doing something wrong? Am I good enough to be here? What is wrong with me? An avalanche of doubt-ridden thoughts crossed my mind as I stared blankly from my desk out the window to Fiftieth Street and Sixth Avenue in Midtown Manhattan, the epicenter of the Big Apple and its endless possibilities. But the once-limitless feeling of success felt fleeting. Instead, on that perfectly beautiful, sunny midsummer afternoon, I wallowed internally in the overly air-conditioned office. It was an especially slow news day, with no meetings to attend and no one at the office for small talk. Just a bunch of open tabs on my desktop staring back at me, which meant plenty of time and stillness to be a prisoner of my own thoughts.

I had started my career as a focused, scrappy production coordinator, and all of a sudden, the ascension to the next step I had always hoped for was here—a promotion to the big-girl job of junior booking producer on a cable news show. It had happened in less than two years. I had jumped from a production role, in which I manned the logistics of a live show in the mornings, to an editorial role, in which I helped identify stories and select corresponding guests or experts, which required me to have more confidence in my ideas and discernment. Yet there I was, a self-conscious mess, battling an internal monologue that I couldn't quite kick to the curb. It was the type of toxic self-talk that wasn't letting me fully step into this role with as much confidence as I knew I had in me.

I sat there at my desk, doing that thing we do where we try to nonsensically fix past scenarios we wish would have gone differently by replaying them in a mental loop. The times I thought I hadn't spoken articulately enough, questioning if I had enough *gravitas*—a word I had suddenly come to know well—to excel in this world of media. I looped mentally through a handful of scenarios at work in which I felt less than confident, questioning my skills for this new position, sending myself into a spiral. Ever since my promotion, something had felt off. I was doing everything to remain in the shadows and downplay this development. I had reverted back to my tried-and-true customer-service mode, putting too much emphasis on getting things "right" instead of making space for what my job actually required: communicating new ideas with authority, building a strong and confident editorial eye, and owning my worth enough to do my job assertively. I was in the trenches of a struggle that is all too familiar to many young women, particularly women of color. I'd put in the work and deserved to be there, so why was I stuck in self-destructive thoughts about my own abilities?

I didn't get it. Like you, I was a go-getter, hardworking and confident enough to get me this far, working at one of the biggest media conglomerates in the world. Yet, in many ways I was led by a nagging fear that the differences between me and the people around me would now be too clear to go unnoticed. Although my first language is Spanish and I learned English early enough in life to lose my accent, I was hard on myself for the way I spoke and how I sometimes mispronounced my words. I still remember the blank stares I received from my college classmates when I pronounced the *s* in Illinois; experiences like these pushed me to constantly monitor my diction and compare my vocabulary to that of everyone else in the newsroom. My feeling of self-reproach at not getting my words "right" turned into a whole story I told myself about my level of intelligence. What started out as simply mispronouncing a few words turned into wondering if my life experiences were too far removed from those of my coworkers, along with a host of other shortcomings that I believed could and would surface if I took up the space that was called for to do my job. I went from zero to one hundred in self-doubt.

The result? I'd stay quiet in meetings for fear of not being articulate or smart enough. I knew intellectually it didn't make sense. I got the job, damn it! But that wasn't enough to make me raise my hand and provide my insight. I even shied away from small talk and opportunities to build rapport with my new colleagues in editorial. My physical, emotional, and intellectual selves weren't coordinating with one another. I had become totally off-balance.

In the emptiness of the expansive office that summer day, I couldn't concentrate. I realized that I had read the same opening passage of a political story five times over. Then the familiar self-reproach and criticism took over—my thoughts became overbearing and spiraled like a never-ending merry-go-round in my mind. I felt bad about feeling bad, because my family and I had sacrificed so much to get me to that coveted spot in my very own cubicle within a mass media and entertainment conglomerate. My parents and siblings had cleaned movie theaters at night while I lay deep asleep in my college dorm room after endless hours of classes and homework. My mom took on double shifts at work despite her arthritis flare-ups just to send bits of cash my way so I could fulfill my version of the American Dream. Deep guilt lodged itself in my mind for feeling so empty and unsettled now that I had "made it." Then shame washed over me. *I have no right to feel this way.* I felt like I had betrayed myself and my family with my own selfish discontentment.

Suddenly, the walls in the office began to close in on me. I jumped out of my chair, grabbed my phone, and rushed to the elevator. I couldn't get out of there fast enough. Through heavy breaths and shaky hands, as I exited the building, I struggled to dial my mom. A sense of impotence surged through me and a golf-ball-sized lump began to form in my throat as I speed-walked across Fifty-First Street with no destination in mind.

Pick up, please pick up.

The outside heat went straight to my head. My rapid-fire heartbeat and tightening chest left me gasping for air. And when I heard my mom's voice on the other end of the line, a stream of uncontrollable tears came rushing down my face. Embarrassed, I tried to find a corner where no one would see me (impossible in the middle of Midtown, by the way).

What is happening to me?

With every passing day since the promotion, my confidence

had begun to slowly dissipate. I couldn't quite put my finger on what was bothering me. I knew in my core that it didn't have to do with my skills or the work at hand, though I had questioned both these things as I wrestled with my self-doubt. When I got down to it, my sudden insecurity was less about my promotion or new job title and more about me in that job title or role. There was a disconnect between how I wanted to show up—or knew I could—and how I was actually showing up at work. I wasn't asserting myself like I knew I could.

What is that sense of doubt that can completely overpower your confidence in certain spaces, especially at work and in places of privilege where you might feel "less than"? *Why* do we feel this way?

These emotions are more common than we imagine. As members of underrepresented communities in the workspace, whether as BIPOCs or immigrants or LGBTQ people, most of the time, we feel like we've worked our butts off to get ourselves in the door and gain access to the type of career opportunities that we've been told by society were not meant for people like us. Many of us have struggled to get a seat at the table or even just a foot in the back of the room. We've had to overcome generational poverty or structural inequities against all odds while learning how to play by the rules of a white world to gain access and inclusion. Stay in your lane, be accommodating, be the yes-girl, overwork yourself until you burn out, be eager but not too eager, show ambition but not too much of it. We read and read, doing research to improve our skills and make ourselves "better" till our eyes burn, scarfing down career advice, whatever we can to carefully strategize our words, appearance, and demeanor so that we can stand out from the pack while also fitting in.

And sometimes it works for us. We get noticed and picked out of a crowd of other employees for being hardworking, always going above and beyond with a positive attitude. (I wrote a whole book on this.) These are the unwritten rules that let any budding employee get ahead in the game. But what happens when you're ready for more? What happens when you're ready for levels that *they* didn't imagine were for you? Or levels where there aren't many people like *you*? And more important, how do you level up when you're ready? How much internal work will it take for you to know, for a fact, that you are ready? To reach the point where you no longer question yourself or need someone else's approval to validate you? Where you know that, even though you're "different," you still belong?

The reality is that part of our value is entrenched in making ourselves useful to others by making their lives easier, allowing our superiors to shine. In a manner of speaking, it's a useful way to learn the ropes at work and do what's expected of us in corporate America when we're starting out. We do the work that our role requires and more without taking up too much space, for fear of feeling like a nuisance or being cast as disruptive. We're *sooo* grateful. We're grateful to have rules to guide us. We're grateful for this opportunity but also scared to lose it. God forbid we lose our chance. So we follow the rules of inclusion that got us noticed, believing they will be equally effective for us in years two, three, and beyond, as our careers grow, as we achieve more and blossom and become prosperous like we're supposed to, because we worked for it...but then we're disappointed. The voices of caution take center stage. *Why do I feel this way?*

Eventually, our titles change and our responsibilities shift, yet we continue to rely on those fundamental rules of inclusion, playing small and "grateful" because that's our safe place. It has helped us snatch and keep what feels like a once-in-a-lifetime opportunity and create a reality that years ago seemed completely inaccessible. If it ain't broke, don't fix it, right? So, even though our positions may now call on us to be bigger, to have own our seat at the table and use it, we continue volunteering to take on tasks or projects below our pay grade. We pick up the slack on the administrative work no one else is doing and hope those around us will take note of the extra hours and careful attention to detail we're putting in—that they'll finally, truly see us, value us, and offer us that raise or promotion we so deserve.

Meanwhile, we don't ask to be in meetings we aren't invited to, even though those meetings may be crucial to our development; instead, we play along with office politics. As the menial tasks pile up on our desk, we begin to wonder about what we should be pushing back on, but these thoughts don't translate into action. Why? We know what we should do: own our greatness. So what's holding us back?

It's a feeling, but we can't quite pinpoint the root cause. We've muted and minimized ourselves from a place so deep inside of us that we literally can't articulate why we're feeling inferior when we know we don't have to. It's an alienation from what we know we deserve. We often don't speak up about it to our peers, even if they can relate, because we think, *How can I even feel this way? I should be grateful.* We should be grateful we're even here to begin with. Done. Although we feel different and carry that sense of not belonging, we cut these thoughts short by sweeping them under the proverbial rug. And we keep going until the next trigger brings it all to the forefront once again. Eventually they can't stay bottled up and manifest themselves in unexpected and unhelpful ways.

The reason behind my full-fledged anxiety attack in the middle of Midtown Manhattan on that sunny afternoon was difficult to understand at first, because it didn't trace back to just one thing. Bubbling up was a confrontation with my old self—the one who found validation in my work through others' approval. I was following a bunch of outdated rules, rules that had once been guiding lights not just on how to navigate the workplace but also on how to navigate life as an undocumented immigrant living in the shadows and growing up in a conservative, majority-white town, reaching for opportunities outside of my societal and economic reality. I was used to feeling like I didn't belong, an outsider waiting to be caught, a DACA recipient proving my worthiness at every turn, an *other*.

My breakdown that day was my very own reflection; as if from a mirror, it was screaming at me that I needed a change. I was Jekyll and Hyde in my own mind, allowing myself to feel these emotions, then scolding myself for them. I knew what I needed to do: step up, find my voice in my role, learn to distinguish myself, stop taking the work dynamics so personally, and get over that feeling of not being good enough. But that was easier said than done. What I really needed was to get to the root of why I wasn't doing that, what was holding me back. And that was more nuanced and complex.

Years later, I'd create Acceso Community during the start of the pandemic, a mentorship program that helps empower women in developing their professional goals, to address this very sentiment. Many of our members are highly educated, determined, hardworking, professional women of color, immigrants, or children of immigrants, who are all bound by a similar predicament. They also feel stuck as they wrestle with a sense of belonging. That affects how we show up at work; it shrinks our greatness. It keeps us from growing and ascending the corporate ladder, or making bigger career moves. We remain reactive instead of purposefully pragmatic. Because of this sense of not belonging, the ladder doesn't tend to feel as safe for us.

Often we are so worried about staying above water, clinging to opportunities and ways to prove ourselves, that we forget to take the time to metabolize what is churning inside us. And even less helpfully, we judge those emotions away. I had grown used to feeling anxious, resentful, and angry about whatever the struggle of the day was, and every time my exasperation culminated in an outburst, my family met me with phrases like "It's not that bad!" "It could be worse!" "*We* had it worse!" That line of thought really did a number on me. Every time I tried to get to the bottom of why I was feeling so helpless, that phrase would play on repeat in my mind: *We had it worse.* It automatically guilted me into dismissing my emotions altogether. Parallel to this was my mom's other favorite phrase when she felt my mind and emotions were spinning into a tornado: "Stop." As if I actually had a choice. As if it were that easy to switch my emotions off at the drop of a hat. "Stop feeling that way," she'd say, and I'd automatically lose it: blood boiling, heart racing, skin crawling, the feeling of being suffocated in my own body.

What she didn't understand, and what I didn't quite grasp either, was that we can't rationalize our way out of our emotions.

By trying to do this, I grew up with the sense that I was too uptight or intense, and that my stress and anxiety were my fault, an inevitable part of my personality. I carried that with me into the workplace, into the anxiety attack on that summer day that jolted me into a sense of awareness.

I've always felt the need to prove myself. Some may call that intense, but I considered it being laser-focused. It made me incredibly good at completing menial tasks, multitasking a million things at once, zipping around as the point person for a three- or sometimes four-hour live news show, being the first one on set at four in the morning during traveling shows, making coffee runs, and staffing talent at the last minute. Being scrappy and preempting everyone's needs in the confines of that job worked well for me. But now, after the promotion, the metrics were blurry. I no longer knew what I had to do to feel needed and validated, and that stopped me from stepping into the power of my new role.

Like many of you reading this, I was the first one in my family to acquire professional success, and there was a mountain of hard work and sacrifice in my rearview mirror that I wasn't willing to put on the line by changing the formula that had gotten me this far. The struggle to get through college without loans or government scholarships as an undocumented student. The time I took off from school to work endless odd jobs. And the collective sweat and tears my family shared to help forge educational opportunities in my path.

Naturally, everything in my mind screamed: *Know your place.* This unassuming phrase perfectly embodies that tug-of-war playing out in our minds each time we feel the need to speak up, do more, take a chance. *Wait, don't do it!* The sense that there is always so much at stake. This is one of the plights of the other in the workplace. Most of us have been following the rules of inclusion for so long that it's almost as if we're waiting for someone to give us permission to stop treading lightly. Yet while we desperately attempt to follow these mandates, we forget about the power we hold in our own voice, and this prevents us from stepping into a fuller version of ourselves.

Sometimes the complications we encounter in showing others our value creep up in the moments when we least expect it, reminding us how different we are. In Acceso Community, many of the women of color talk about how their sense of inadequacy in the workplace—which is tied to their background, ethnicity, or identity—flares up every time they find themselves pressured to fit in and belong.

Janelle, a young woman who grew up in a modest household and was the first of her family to go to college, recently shared with me that she automatically tensed up and felt adrenaline rush through her gut every time partners at her law firm made small talk about the fabulous time they had hitting the slopes in Aspen or lounging by the pool at their summer homes in the Hamptons. She'd smile along, nodding "knowingly," while racking her mind for something she could contribute so as to belong to this group of colleagues whose backgrounds were far removed from hers. But she feared that whatever she did share might pronounce her otherness, since her reality, lifestyle, and appearance—she was often the lone Black woman in the group—fell on the opposite side of the spectrum from those of the mainly well-off white men holding these chats.

Could she talk about how her weekend escapes were actually trips to her childhood home to check up on her parents, who were struggling with their health and could barely make ends meet? Or that in lieu of a summer abroad while she was in college—often a fun topic among younger staffers at her firm—she had been working side gigs to afford going back to school? No. She believed that mentioning any of this would only expand the divide between her and them. There were moments when she spent so much time focused on how to respond that she avoided opportunities to interact and network with the same ease as her coworkers. So she got used to sinking into the safety of silence.

Janelle's story really hit home for me, because I know that woozy feeling all too well, and I'm sure you do too. Many of us have been in a situation—a meeting, a networking event—where we have something to say, but like Janelle, we stop ourselves, fearing what people might think. These feelings may be as much about our self-limiting beliefs as they are about our work environments. If we don't identify and process why we're feeling this way, they will continue to surface and result in unintended consequences, draining us and getting in the way of our confidence, and the ease we need to show up with more authority and self-assuredness in our jobs.

The old saying goes, *It's not personal, it's work.* Business is business, right? But if you feel different, like you don't fully belong, it can be difficult to discern whether you're reacting to an uncomfortable work scenario at face value or projecting a lived experience of exclusion onto it. Is it really "not personal" all the time?

For women of color, sometimes or often, it is.

One day, Frances, an Asian American media industry colleague of mine, sat at her desk, and, as on any other morning at the entertainment magazine she worked at, the ten or so coworkers surrounding her cubicle made small talk that flowed throughout the office. She doesn't remember the exact conversation that preceded the comment that would pierce her psyche from there on out, only the knee-jerk-reaction croak she uttered when she heard: "You look like a beautiful china doll." This tone-deaf comment, intended to be a *compliment*, came from none other than her manager—the person who was supposed to advocate for Frances at work and serve as her career mentor. It stung like hell, though. And she dwelled on it for months on end, rearing its head to remind her, in case she forgot: *You are different.*

Every time she needed that extra boost of confidence to feel safe, heard, respected, and equal enough to raise her hand and exchange creative ideas, it was flattened by that inner voice: *You are different.* Being Asian American felt more salient than what she could offer—it was as if she'd been reduced and exoticized. That made it harder for her to contribute in work environments that called for her to put herself out there and advocate effectively for her ideas. She also felt restrained from doing things that had the potential to add value to the team and her career in new ways. What's more, when her manager made this off-color remark, she added, "You know what I mean," doubling down on her comment and, in a way, asking Frances to buy into it and agree to be on her side. All the while, Frances was mired in embarrassment and pain. If she had any doubt that her race, in one way or another, made her different, it was gone now.

How do you bounce back from a situation like that and reclaim your power? That's something we will explore together in the following chapters, because it's going to take more than one paragraph to get to the bottom of these feelings and finally flip the script. And that we will do.

Kenji Yoshino, a professor at New York University School of Law and the director of their Center for Diversity, Inclusion, and Belonging, has written extensively about the concept of "covering." The term was coined in 1963 by sociologist Erving Goffman to describe how individuals with stigmatized identities "make a great effort to keep the stigma from looming large." When such stigma shows up in the workplace, it can have lasting negative consequences on the individuals doing the covering in order to fit in and get ahead. There are a million ways we use covering to play down our differences and limit bringing our full selves to work. This not only has a negative impact on our well-being but also affects our sense of self-worth.

When your basic needs depend so much on your environment and they aren't met, it can leave you feeling deprived, helpless, frustrated, angry, and unmotivated. Covering happens for a multitude of reasons—a toxic environment, a boss who lacks proper management training, microaggressions, workplace injustice, and the list goes on. We could spend all day calling out and naming the (very real) outside factors that stand in the way of our success. But to step into our power and find our voices professionally, we need to retrace where, how, and in what ways our voices have been muted. We need to come face-to-face with what we've been repressing in our attempts to keep up with the rules of inclusion that have helped us survive. Along with that, we need to learn to push back in real time and keep track of our messaging in order to take back power at work and truly embrace being the only and/or the first in those roles. This will eventually allow us to create new, more equitable rules that open the playing field and pull others up along with us!

If you are an immigrant, a first- or second-generation American, a minority, or someone who simply didn't grow up feeling like you had access to many opportunities, the road to an equal playing field can feel like a constant uphill battle. It can seem lonely and even helpless. The support you wish you had doesn't exist. Starting out, I did the best I could in the only way I knew how: staying endlessly busy, thinking and rethinking ways to make small opportunities and what-ifs turn into something—anything. Instead of sitting still and succumbing to my environment, I focused on the swim upstream while also trying my hardest to remain in the shadows and avoid exposing even a hint of my undocumented status. That was an internal battle I faced all on my own.

These emotions can weigh heavy on our existence. We've spent so much time covering, trying to fit in, looking endlessly for ways to belong, and downplaying differences we've convinced ourselves could work against us, that we haven't put as much attention on how to ask for more. And if you're reading this, chances are you're ready for more—more room to make a difference, more money, more responsibility, more advocating power for yourself and others. You're ready for the real you to show up and play *big*.

So forget being grateful, forget being "found out," forget feeling different. It's time to show up as someone more authentic and aligned with who you are, and to uncover how to make your biggest strengths work for you. This is the key to unlocking the next level of your career.

Because if there is one truth I've learned, it's this: We have the power to choose how to deal with it all. We can either believe the lousy cards we were handed are part of our narrative or opt for an alternative.

That doesn't mean that alternative has to be crystal clear. While it might often feel like we're walking through a fog, there is power and deeper self-trust to be gained if we choose the slow and steady approach. If we choose to do this our way, not abiding by the old rules or what other people have done before but operating as the authentic and beautifully unique people we are. That is what I hope we'll be able to accomplish together. With this book, I hope to build a community of people who learn how to trust themselves enough to reach a clearing in their seemingly nebulous path. I want you to embrace your differences and learn how to use them effectively in your favor—to stand out, to make yourself indispensable, and to lean into that advantage of being different. Yes! It is an *advantage*! Let's learn to see it that way. Bringing greater awareness to our behavior and the behavior of others in the workplace is the first step to figuring out how we can evolve internally to soar externally in our careers. Don't lose sight of your convictions. You're the agent of change in your own life. Let's get to work.

3

When the Other Was Born

The lights of Studio 1A shone brightly overhead. My mind raced to concentrate on what was going to come out of my mouth next. Would I be able to get the words out? *Oh God, Daniela, please don't fuck this up,* I thought as I sat next to Mika Brzezinski, cohost of MSNBC's *Morning Joe* and my mentor. We were seconds away from being interviewed live by Savannah Guthrie on the *Today* show about the book we had coauthored, *Earn It! Know Your Value and Grow Your Career, in Your 20s and Beyond.*

Three, two, one... Savannah introduced us and our book cover flashed across a screen. I glanced over at Mika. She gave me an encouraging *I'm proud of you* look, and I smiled back at her confidently. My nerves unexpectedly subsided. It was go time.

This was my first TV appearance, one that would kick off a national press tour for our book and open the doors for me to connect with thousands of young women who felt drawn to my story as an immigrant—undocumented at that—who struggled to get her foot in the door without any connections and somehow managed to rise through the ranks of MSNBC and collaborate with a nationally renowned journalist, TV host, and author, in a book about how women can know and grow their value at the beginning of their careers. More than once while writing the book, I had thought, *I'm just getting started with my own career. Who am I to tell other women how to develop theirs?* But like many other women—particularly women of color who bear the added burden of systemic inequalities—I knew enough about how to roll up my sleeves, get the work done, and channel the grit that's the product of our hardships into action and solutions. That's essentially how I had reached this moment despite my lack of access.

And here I was, living the dream at MSNBC in New York City, with a book tour underway.

But feeling at ease in this new space and believing that others would see the value in my knowledge was requiring me to own my power, and I knew that I needed to do more than just roll up my sleeves if I wanted to operate on a higher level—I needed to get to the root of the thing that had filled me with hesitancy from the get-go and urged me to proceed with caution. I had to grapple with unresolved issues around my sense of belonging.

Belonging is a communal space, we're told. It's a connecting factor that makes us feel at ease, *safe.* When we feel like we fit into our work environments, we're able to do better work; we feel appreciated and a little more inclined to put ourselves out there as we are.

I'm lucky to say that I've had an incredible mentor like Mika who's encouraged me to own my story. I say that acknowledging that the reality for minorities in the workplace is that many professional environments are far from celebrating our differences. This means we're often spending most of our time and energy desperately searching for belonging, and it drives us to change pieces of who we are to feel like we're part of the community. We do this not because we want to or because we dislike our authentic selves but to succeed, to do what we came to accomplish, to develop our careers, to reach our potential, to break the glass ceiling, and to sit at the table. And for us there are unique barriers that get in the way: prejudices and underlying biases that still exist in the workplace, along with the feeling of unease that comes from being "the only" or "the other." From the urge to tweak what we say for fear of being called aggressive to the act of simply downplaying who we are for fear of not being well received, there is often an overall difficulty in feeling at ease or safe.

"Safety" takes on a whole new meaning at work. It means that you feel safe communicating with and even challenging others, and feel a level of comfort knowing that you won't be penalized, judged, or discredited for doing so. In a 1999 journal article, leadership scholar Amy Edmondson used the term "psychological safety" to refer to the "shared belief held by members of a team that the team is safe for interpersonal risk-taking." This condition leads to more engaging collaboration, a greater flow of innovative ideas, and an overall healthier and happier place to work.

While many employers want to believe this exists in their workplaces, we know that's not always the case. In fact, it's likely *not* the case for underrepresented groups. How can you feel safe if you've had experience being racialized by your skin color or stigmatized by your background? It's hard to fully self-actualize and achieve your potential when you're squarely focused on surviving, minimizing, shielding, hiding parts of yourself, and constantly monitoring what you say and how you say it. Making yourself heard and taking up space is difficult when there's a lack of psychological safety. Instead of being part of a team where you feel empowered to collaborate and contribute, you feel excluded.

In response, our instinct is to recoil. We may opt not to speak up when we disagree or have a different perspective from everyone else in the office—even one that would add more value or insight—for fear of being perceived as the "angry" Black woman, the overly emotional Latina, or the Asian woman who shouldn't be breaking the "submissive" stereotype. Our silence in these scenarios seeks to fill our own need for psychological safety. Stereotypes can hang over our head in ways that threaten our ability to feel comfortable being ourselves in the same ways that, say, a white man or, in many cases, a white woman does. If you're perceived as too bold or too intimidating, you can often be met with contempt. If you've got a seat at the table and find yourself being the *only* woman, person of color, immigrant, or any type of minority, it can be hard, lonely, and alienating. So we learn to adapt, to fit in, to assimilate to create our own sense of safety. And we succeed, only to realize that much of our uniqueness might have been compromised along the way.

We could focus solely on the people and places that keep us excluded, but if we're going to change things on our watch—without waiting for the rest of the world to catch up—we'll need to do some digging into the development of our own identities and the belief systems we've created around them. To get a handle on what we're feeling now, first we need to go back to where it all began. We've had to work with the challenges of otherness our whole lives, but in the workplace they feel magnified, because our time, money, contributions, power to make a difference, and ability to follow our passions are on the line. Belonging can feel crucial to our success, yet our battle to *earn our spot* started long before the workplace.

I spent the first ten years of my life moving from one part of the world to another too many times. My young parents were struggling to find a better life for their kids, but the constant uprooting left us with inconsistent housing and no real sense of community, which meant I was brought up in a chaotic household where the ever-present goal was to stay afloat. Then, when I was eleven and we finally put down roots in Ohio, I had to learn how to walk the tightrope between my Chilean origins and the American culture into which I yearned to assimilate. The unintended by-product of that process was that I became quieter, feeling the push and pull of what people assumed of me versus who I really was, and began to adapt my personality and voice to resemble my new surroundings. I became a sponge to my environment, constantly searching for clues on how to act, react, and interact in order to feel like I was on equal footing with everyone else.

As the years went by, my identity was muddied not only by the versions of myself I had made to fit everyone's expectations but also by the feeling of being "Latina but not Latina enough," or feeling American despite the constant reminders that I was not. In short, no matter what I did, I still didn't truly belong. But as I chugged along, I continued to bury any sense of limiting beliefs that cropped up and desperately looked for distractions. I focused on my path, on college, on internships, and then on my long-awaited career. I was convinced that burying myself in achievement and validation would take care of all of this.

One night, after another long, grueling workday at 30 Rockefeller Plaza booking guests for *Morning Joe*, then writing a piece for NBC News's Know Your Value, and finally ending the day editing my column for *Cosmopolitan* magazine, I came home to my Williamsburg studio apartment to find my dog begging for affection. Exhausted, I reached for a late-night snack, popping open my laptop to finish up some work. As I combed through unread emails, my eyes landed on one from an unknown sender with the subject line YOUR UPCOMING TRIP TO LIMA.

That's weird, I thought. I did have an upcoming trip to my Ohio hometown, but this wasn't the person I had been corresponding with about the book signing that a local women's empowerment group was holding for me there. The group had invited me to speak about *Earn It!* as a homecoming of sorts, and that night, the local news in my hometown had run a spot advertising the event and my backstory—how I went from being a small-town undocumented girl to being a national cable news producer and best-selling author. In all honesty, I felt a bit uneasy about going back home after coming out of the shadows as undocumented for the first time in public. But I shook that feeling off. After all, this was not intended to be a political conversation. It was my chance to talk about my book and help women own their value, take the reins of their careers, and advocate for more for themselves. I was excited about the conversation to be had with women who wanted and needed to hear that message.

When I clicked open the email and began reading the words on my computer screen, my chest tightened.

As was broadcast on the local news this evening, January 9, Sally Chester was interviewed as hosting you, an illegal immigrant at the Bistro restaurant. This invitation was acknowledged to promote your status as an illegal alien—not undocumented—illegal.

You are therefore a criminal and not welcome in Lima or Ohio or in this country…you are ILLEGAL.

DG

A legal citizen, born and raised in Ohio

Unfortunately, this rhetoric was nothing new. I had heard this type of disparaging comment toward immigrants before and had been working long enough in media to know that the woman who had sent this email was a troll—someone with too much time (and utter ignorance) on her hands. So my initial reaction was to brush it off. Who the hell would care so much about going after an author's book signing when the book aimed to empower young women? But the sting I felt about being called out as "illegal"—as if I weren't even a person—lingered.

My mind raced with questions as I tried to process what I had just read. I heard this message before; from white guys on cable news with national platforms to people in my own hometown, and now, when I thought I was way past all of that, there it was again, in bold letters on my screen.

What followed that night as I sat in my apartment alone was a series of wild emotions I had little control over: Outrage. Sadness. Then anger. I'd take a deep breath to calm myself down, only to be hit by another wave of feelings, until one began to take center stage: fear. Yet as I crawled into bed hoping to get some sleep, I couldn't help but think, *Wait, what am I afraid of?*

My media career had exposed me to all kinds of vitriol and a handful of hate crimes I wish I could unsee: protests in the name of ethnic superiority and horrible acts of hate, racism, prejudice, and bias that we all know too well, which have taken so many innocent lives and led to ugly manifestos trying to show people of different races, ethnicities, sexual preferences, and belief systems that they don't belong. It's hard to pretend these digs at your identity, your race, your background, yourself don't affect you personally. That small piece of hate mail made me question whether I should go through with this book event at all. Would I need some type of security? This was 2019; the political climate wasn't exactly the most conducive to tolerance. Would there be hecklers? Could I emotionally separate this from the work I was there to do?

Finally I realized that although that disturbing letter was an attempt to bring me down, humiliate me, and undermine me, it also did something surprisingly useful. It brought a subconscious limiting belief to the surface that I wasn't good enough to be in this country. I was a confident young author who'd managed to climb up the ranks in media. *I was good enough.* I knew that. Why, then, did I suddenly have a flood of memories of times I felt otherwise? The *you don't belong here* voice that had followed me my entire life in the United States suddenly stared me straight in the face in the form of what I assumed this woman to look like: a total "Karen."

I would never give that person the satisfaction of receiving a response, but I barely slept that night.

I started to doubt myself. *Should I cancel the event?* I questioned whether the event or my appearance had any value. This wasn't about the letter; it was about the narrative I had subconsciously told about myself to myself. Though I was reacting to societal beliefs and a troll, I'd gotten really good at looking at myself through the eyes of someone else, for better or for worse.

If I continued to buy into the message this troll had sent my way, I would've allowed ignorance, bias, and prejudice to win, to dictate my next move and, in part, my own professional choices. And there was no way in hell that was happening. In order to move past these limiting thoughts and take power back, I had to stop and recognize the dynamics at play here. Someone felt threatened by my identity, and that brought to the surface my own subconscious beliefs that I was not good enough to belong.

Mine wasn't a solely personal predicament; it is a common one that many of us go through on an individual level. How do we create space for our own identity without being dragged down by the interpretations, expectations, or limitations others place on us? We can't always brush things off or not take them personally, as we often attempt to do at work. Sometimes it's not just what's happening in the moment that makes it harder for us to push through to the other side; it's also the weight of the memories triggered by these circumstances, the tugging at our sense of self and questioning of our worth.

In order to confront this, I had to take myself out of the equation momentarily and observe what I was feeling at the moment, looking at my own life as if it were a movie I was watching about someone else. I had to identify where I began to *believe* in the experiences or scenarios that left me feeling undermined. What did this lady trigger that was festering under the surface?

When you take the time to sit down and really think about the honest answers to these questions, it's likely you'll find it wasn't just one person or one thing. The accumulation of prejudice we've experienced throughout our lives turns into self-limiting beliefs we internalize in order to ascend. After all, that piece of hate mail wasn't the first time I was made to feel less than. Nevertheless, it caused the floodgates to burst wide open. Memories that I had tucked away in my subconscious, the times when I had felt like the other, started pouring into my mind.

Growing up, I did not belong. Not on paper, not in the system, and not in my environment.

The word "undocumented" is more than a status; it's a feeling. It's a constant state of being, and it was always there with me. Am I enough? Am I worthy? I was not alone in this feeling, but in my case, there was supporting evidence that made it harder not to take those thoughts as factual. I lacked the very paperwork that validated my belonging in this country. I was in total limbo without a path forward. Whatever inadequacies I felt were compounded by my lack of status. So I built up a shell to protect me from the prejudice I encountered in my small town, and I learned to bury my voice—to accommodate, explain, and appease. It was a coping mechanism that I absorbed early on, which quickly spilled over into areas of my life where I felt like I had to work hard to prove myself.

One of these experiences that stayed with me was when I met my then-boyfriend's parents as a teen. No matter who you are, meeting a partner's parents for the first time can be nerve-racking. I wanted to do my best to make a good first impression for many reasons. He had a big, close-knit family like mine, but his upbringing was vastly different from my own. He had grown up in the same town all his life and had conservative, well-educated parents who had gone to top-ranked schools. They were well off and well known in town, the sort of parents who were at every one of their kids' games and recitals, and could comfortably clock out of their nine-to-five jobs to enjoy family meals. This was a stark contrast to my immigrant parents, who worked two or three shifts and came home, on a good day, by eight at night with a bucket of Lee's chicken, which each kid would eat on their own schedule because our parents were too exhausted to impose rules about family mealtimes.

I was scheduled to meet my boyfriend's family for dinner at one of the best restaurants in town. Blood rushed to my cheeks as my family dropped me off in our station wagon. I was late. My dad had fallen behind schedule, struggling to start the car engine on his way home from his factory job across town.

"Here is fine!" I blurted before we neared the restaurant's front door, my mind swirling with the thought that this was the first impression I'd have to lead with.

"Good luck!" yelled my twelve-year-old brother from the back seat through a devilish grin and a big cackle. Even at his age, he knew I was walking into a minefield. I rolled my eyes and hoped the loud creak of the old car door closing couldn't be heard inside.

As I stepped into the Italian restaurant, I quickly spotted my boyfriend and his whole family on the left, already sitting at the table, and watched as all of their eyes turned my way. I walked toward them knowing I would be vetted, almost expecting that they already had some sort of preconceived judgment about my immigrant roots, but I figured if I played my cards right, they'd overlook the cultural and socioeconomic gaps between us.

After apologizing profusely for being late, I took my seat and exchanged small talk over appetizers. With the main course, lasagna, came the usual softballs: "How is school going?" "What was it like growing up in Chile?" And I was batting like a champ, or so I thought. Until his mother threw the ultimate curveball.

"So, are you an alien? I mean...do you have a green card?" Her eyes were locked on me as she fumbled through this question. And for an instant, I stopped breathing. The inquisition hit me like a pile of rocks. My thoughts reeled. *What do I say? How can I answer this and still be in her good graces? Will they accept me if I tell them the truth?*

"Well—I..."

I felt totally blindsided.

"Oh my God, Mom! No, she's an illegal alien!" offered one of my boyfriend's brothers sarcastically, as if coming to my rescue.

"What a question!" followed his father, as everyone joined in and laughed it all off, delighting themselves in the bluntness of the question that so obviously did not need to be answered.

As I smiled along with them, playing into their assumption

that I was not undocumented, a strange out-of-body sensation came over me, as if I were two separate people digesting my environment. The confident version of me pretended that this outright biased comment had little to no effect on the expertly disguised other version of me, who was screaming at me in my mind to run away before I got caught.

When I came back from what felt like a mental blackout, I found the confident person in me take over. *Keep calm.* I explained my immigration status by lying to appease them, telling them that my paperwork was in process or something. I fought every inch of my gut and soul from disclosing the truth. As I scrambled to find a way to ease their doubts about my legal status, I was unintentionally feeding into their bias and also internalizing it. It was one of the first times I remember feeling deep shame. Even so, I self-soothed, conditioning my body and words to deflect this uncomfortable feeling of inadequacy, and carried on.

In my mind, my boyfriend's mother's message was clear: *You don't belong.* It felt like she had already made up her mind before even taking the chance to get to know me. I'm sure you can relate on some level, especially if, like me, you grew up in a community where you stuck out like a sore thumb. I began to believe that I needed to adapt by appeasing whatever doubts, worries, or hesitancies might come up about me and my background. After all, these were good, community- and family-oriented, churchgoing people. *It must not be them,* I told myself. *It's me. I* needed to work harder to assimilate and earn their trust.

This uncomfortable dinner situation was the first time I felt the threat of what being "the other" meant to a group in which family, friends, and acquaintances, for the most part, all looked the same. Those hegemonic communities have grown used to the consistency that comes from the lack of diversity within their close circles. I can imagine people's skin crawled in my town at the thought that I might be "illegal," but I needed more years to process and fully understand how their bias likely came from simple lack of exposure to someone different from them.

Of course people are unfamiliar with things they haven't encountered before, but to wholeheartedly judge, dismiss, or reject, well, that's bias in a nutshell, if not outright bigotry. It's the fear of the unknown. It may have helped ease my stress if I had understood this back then, but all I knew was that I was the odd one out, someone they couldn't quite put their finger on, and deep down inside, that dissonance probably scared them. This made me harbor shame about my very identity. I didn't have anyone like me in my corner to encourage me or teach me how to handle that emotion. My family was likely dealing with their own repressed emotions, and were also much too worried about getting food on our table to think about *feelings*.

That relationship was short-lived (shocker, I know). But this memory remained in my subconscious for years, rearing its ugly head on other occasions where I faced my socioeconomic limits when trying to make it into rooms where I felt like I didn't belong. *You are illegal!* it yelled at me, making me feel like a total fraud.

What I didn't know back then was that I was not "illegal"; I was undocumented. I also didn't know that calling me or anyone in my circumstance an "alien" carried an enormous psychological weight. Currently, there is legislation introduced in Congress that would remove the word "alien" from US immigration laws and replace it with "noncitizen." Immigration activists, legal scholars, and others have taken issue with the term "alien," saying it downplays the importance of the role immigrants have had historically in the United States, from the European immigrants who colonized it to the enslaved Africans who were forced to immigrate against their will. However you want to look at it, the term holds one unchallengeable message for those on the receiving end: that we are foreign, outsiders, *other*. We feel the force of its psychological weight. That one measly word dangled over us has the power to make us question ourselves, our identities, and our place in the world. This epithet translates into a rejection that tells us that our inherent being is not good enough, is not worthy, does not and will never belong. We exist "illegally" in places where we contribute, build communities, volunteer in religious spaces, and pay taxes for welfare and health care that we ourselves cannot use. "Illegals" like us shouldn't exist…yet we do.

But back then, I didn't know how out of line it was to slide that question to a teenage girl already drowning in nerves over what was supposed to be a friendly family meal. I didn't have that discernment yet. I was used to the judgments, the probing questions, the short-sighted jokes that came my way. The "wetback" comments. The laughs that were shared over signature phrases like "Those damn illegals!" To me, it was the reality that I had to learn to live in. My annoyance and anger over being in the shadows only translated to shame over my situation. I knew none of this was right, but I didn't know how to process it or articulate it, so I just played along to fit in, to not get caught, to go unnoticed, to make that part of me seemingly disappear. I fought to shed that sense of otherness, to not let it swallow me whole.

It took me years to dig through the internalized bias I had stashed away, to understand what terms like "illegal alien" symbolized and the negative connotations they held and still hold. It's dehumanizing. And it further exacerbates the shame and blame we spend years trying to undo. Any lingering doubts about whether my feelings at the time were justified were laid to rest recently by an old classmate, who happened to be one of the few people of color in our class, when they told me in conversation, "My parents always stood up for you when they heard racist remarks about you, your family, or anyone else." I decided not to follow up on exactly what those comments were. But, yes, the bias that I felt was real, even though I had chosen to ignore it in self-defense... to survive in that environment. As different as my family was, I was determined not to let myself feel less than anyone else. At least not in public. Some small part of me knew that our differences are actually what make us unique, eclectic, and interesting. But that voice of reason was just a whisper back then.

The interesting thing about bias is that it doesn't just happen *to* us. I'm sure most of us notice that same bias within our families and communities too. We've heard our uncles, aunts, or grandparents say something that was off-color or racist, and everyone just kind of laughed it off.

In unspoken ways, I was taught it was safer to stay in my lane. After I broke up with the boyfriend in the story above, my grandmother and mom made brutally honest comments about my relationship like, "It would have never worked out. The family would never have accepted you." God love our Latina mothers and their no-holds-barred remarks and (at times unsolicited) counsel. Comments like these were meant to be supportive, but they were also unknowingly emphasizing that the bias I had experienced had no remedy, because no matter what I might have done, *they* wouldn't have accepted *me*. This made my efforts to adjust and fit in all the harder, because my family was unwittingly teaching me that all of this was a result of our circumstances and therefore, in some ways, my identity. They perpetuated and upheld my own sense of otherness.

I now realize those comments had less to do with me and more to do with them grappling with their own setbacks, revealing their worry and inherent need to protect me from the very bias they knew existed and perhaps even experienced themselves, both in the United States and in Chile. Because class divide, prejudice, and racism aren't just an American thing. The need to belong and make those who are different from the status quo feel like they don't belong is universal, and it seeps into every part of our world. But the effect it has on us can vary greatly, given something as simple as the color of our skin.

And yes, this opens up a whole other can of worms that needs to be addressed within our immigrant and minority communities. We still have work to do to dismantle the issues surrounding colorism, which remains prevalent in our native countries. Even the "good immigrant" narrative fails to consider how factors like systemic racism and its ties to generational poverty affect our communities. But being open to talking about it is the first step to, at the very least, trying to understand our varied experiences.

I think it's absolutely fair to say that my sister, who inherited beautiful dark-skinned genes from our Haitian grandfather, has an added layer of bias to deal with. I am light-skinned. Although I've had many barriers to overcome, including my undocumented status, socioeconomic background, and lack of networks and mentors growing up, I realize that I have benefited from the privilege of having fairer skin. I will never fully know the additional prejudice my sister has encountered and will encounter for the rest of her personal and professional life simply because of the color of her skin. I've had to face the question *"What* are you?" far less often than my sister, and other race-based slights like being seated last at a restaurant because of the color of my skin.

Growing up, the sense of rejection, isolation, and otherness became so overwhelming for my sister that, while I did everything in my power to be involved in as many extracurriculars as possible at our private school, she begged to be pulled out of there, her darker complexion and bigger curves falling in stark contrast with the skinnier white girls on her softball team. She chose to withdraw rather than fight to achieve some form of assimilation and opted instead for a smaller public high school that she hoped might be a better fit. The latter had its consequences; it didn't provide the same type of college prep courses, opportunities, or exposure to families that pushed their kids toward higher education. So it didn't come as a surprise that after graduation, my sister felt lost when it came to her next steps and eventually opted to matriculate in online courses at a community college—a contrast to my own path.

The systemic and cultural factors at play as we grow up in a system that constantly works against us undeniably shape and affect our own beliefs about ourselves, which we have to work hard to dispel. To this day, my sister feels torn about her future. She has hopes to develop her own photography business and strike out on her own, but the very steps of finding mentorship and learning experiences in that field are riddled with socioeconomic and cultural obstacles, on top of her own self-doubts about how to get there. She is still working on overcoming the difficulties she faced growing up in spaces she felt alienated from.

I realize that there were more factors at play that made our experiences so different, including our personalities, but my sister's case undoubtedly exemplifies why many people feel like the other. Factor in the day-to-day, real-life whispers, microaggressions, and internalized bias, and otherness becomes an uphill battle. Ultimately, living through prejudice because of your skin tone, nationality, documentation status, socioeconomic class, education level, background, religious beliefs, or sexual orientation has lasting results on your sense of self. Instead of leaning into and loving our differences, our early memories of feeling like an other can have such a lasting impact that they make us feel like our uniqueness is a liability. Carrying around these limiting beliefs directly affects how we define who we are, who we want to be, and how we present ourselves to the world.

This came to light for me recently in a conversation with Nina, one of my mentees at Acceso. I was giving her advice on tactics for effective networking—more specifically how to introduce herself and her work confidently, clearly, and concisely to new professional contacts. I could see her getting frustrated at the task, and she finally blurted, "I can't." She insisted she needed more time to think and practice. After several sessions in which she gave the same excuse, I suspected there was something more there about the way she viewed herself that she likely wasn't even aware of.

It wasn't that she didn't have the experience or didn't have impressive credentials to share. On the contrary, she was an executive assistant to high-level global executives in a major media company, and had plenty to say about what she did and how she did it. Everything about her gave the impression that she was a self-confident person with a type A personality who paid attention to important details and had a strong work ethic—perfect qualities for someone in a high-level executive administrative role. Yet when it came time to turn the tables and talk up her value, she couldn't articulate her strengths. It was like the words got stuck in her throat. Instead, whenever she had an opportunity to network, she'd find herself subconsciously accommodating others by asking tons of questions about them, leaving no time to actually talk about herself.

So, rather than pushing her to do it, I started to help her explore the belief systems she was raised on and how she related to others. What started out as a conversation on how to practically and tactically network with others ended up being more of a personal examination of what was holding her back from talking about herself. We found helpful clues that explained the origins of this behavior. She was the youngest of five children, and every time she spoke out of turn at the dinner table, her immigrant parents reprimanded her. These types of experiences ingrained in her that she had to "know her place" in order not to be "disruptive." This, in turn, made her feel like she had to constantly stay in her lane and be conscious of being respectful and obliging to others, especially to her "superiors." The belief system she had constructed was that it was safer to say nothing at all, unless someone else specifically asked her to express herself.

This way of relating to others didn't stay at the dinner table. It followed her into many other facets of her life as a Black woman navigating the nuances of coming from an immigrant family in a small town, and ultimately it followed her into her career. And it backfired in her professional life. She kept hearing that questioning voice: *Is what I have to say good enough to be shared?* That voice became a permanent loop in her mind. You may think this is a normal thought to have, especially if you're just starting and figuring out the social and environmental clues around you. I agree; this is what I did too. But the problem was that it became her default thinking, especially when talking about herself to professionals several rungs above her. She struggled to do so with ease.

Her sense of value came from a sense of accommodation—there was safety in hunkering down and doing the work others needed. You can imagine how this way of thinking might derail her when it came to getting to the next level of her career, participating in negotiations, and ultimately vying for leadership roles. Because her deep-rooted beliefs were holding her back from really taking more power at work, Nina needed to peel away at the layer that was buried under all those thoughts that led her to second-guess herself. She had to unlearn the schemas she had learned as a child of immigrant parents that kept her in that "safe" zone where if she didn't have the perfect answer, she might as well not say anything at all.

Nina isn't an isolated case. It's not easy to dismantle what we've learned at home, which can be compounded in social settings and places of work, and which may even serve us in certain ways. While my experience is different from Nina's, they're both examples of how we create many of our beliefs about ourselves through other people's reactions. If we buy into them enough, they can easily develop into self-limiting beliefs that affect our worth and value. The limiting belief I created was that I wasn't enough until I proved myself—not just to myself but to others as well. For Nina, the dynamic at home that spilled over at work whenever she felt her race (African American), gender (she was one of the only women in the room), or age (she was one of the youngest on the team) taught her that she should avoid looking or sounding unintelligent at all costs. *Better to know your place.* So, many times, she'd say nothing at all.

But we're never going to say the perfect thing at the perfect time, because perfection doesn't exist. And we need to know just how much we risk losing if we allow those limiting beliefs to lead us. They shrink, confine, and mute us, yet we fixate on keeping those beliefs because they may have once worked for us. Nina kept the peace at home by "knowing her place," while I found safety in the validation I got from my achievements. Both tendencies we brought with us to the workplace.

And why wouldn't we? At MSNBC and as an author, I suddenly had access to opportunities I didn't even imagine were possible. I didn't want to mess it up by changing my whole approach. We can't afford to let internalized bias or limiting beliefs interfere as we chart a path toward success. We've got to gather enough courage to raise our hand and speak the truth in a room of people, even if we were taught to stay in our place. And we should never be ashamed of our religion, ethnicity, disability, socioeconomic status, or whatever difference society has told us to be ashamed of. Think about how many successes we could take hold of as individuals, families, and communities if we were to break free from the bias holding us down. We'd be able to leap toward uncharted territories and live outside of what others have told us is the realm of possibility for our careers.

If you've grown up in an environment where beliefs about your own community, family, or identity were limited, boxed in, or stereotyped, there is unlearning to be done. That can be hard when the very members of that community, especially in your own family, have subconsciously projected those limiting beliefs onto you. It's not an easy realization, and there are uncomfortable conversations that go with it, but we must bring self-awareness to the fact that we've opted into ideas about ourselves to maintain the status quo, to feel like we belong or at least try to gain equal footing. In that self-awareness we can find clarity on how to act differently and acknowledge where we ourselves might have perpetuated or even exacerbated prejudice. Identifying these belief systems, understanding where they come from, and becoming self-aware is the first step to taking back your power.

Belonging does not necessarily have to precede success. Our internalized ideas about the limitations, stereotypes, or prejudice we feel from others are not accurate reflections of our capabilities or the opportunities available to us. When I identified my own internalized bias about being undocumented, I realized that I was actually fighting self-imposed restrictions and limitations. Obstacles and constraints of all kinds will come and go in our lives; the key is to acknowledge their presence and decide how long we want them to live in our heads.

You have the power to make shortcomings part of your narrative or to decide otherwise. I started by asking myself these questions: Where am I mentally allowing bias to fast-forward to a "no" or an "I can't"? Where am I taking bias down, refusing it, getting to my "Yes, thank you very much," and taking my piece of the pie? And because I have to live in this society, where I *expect* bias and judgment, how much of my own reality will I let someone else dictate from their vantage point rather than choosing to stick to my own vantage point?

Make room for a mentality that doesn't require the permission of others. Don't stay in your lane. Rewrite the script.

Knowing I had the power to choose my narrative opened up a world of possibility. And although that possibility may be hindered by real outside factors and barriers, as you've seen in my case and likely also experienced firsthand, changing the way you think about yourself and allowing yourself to take up more space, no matter if it's a perfect fit, is the first step to changing your outer world and determining your own success.

So go ahead, think about the times you've felt you had to appease, change, mold, or pivot what you really wanted to say or do in an attempt to make others feel comfortable. List them out. Go as far back as you can remember and trace the origins of your behavior. Was your limiting belief system playing a part in molding your behavior in order to fit into a box that felt unnatural to you?

I feel I will be judged. I started to feel this way when . . .
I feel I can't do this. I started to feel this way when . . .
I feel I will be alienated. I started to feel this way when . . .
I feel I will be rejected. I started to feel this way when . . .

Now that you've identified some of the beliefs that keep you stuck in a loop, and where they might have originated from, set a new belief system that takes you out of that mindset and replaces it with action-driven statements to help get you there.

> *I am safe taking up space as I am. Going forward, I will not stay quiet for fear of criticism if I have something of value to add, because I know my wholeness is important and valuable.*
>
> *I can do this. Going forward, I will be aware of why I'm feeling doubtful and hesitant and realize that it may be working against my growth.*
>
> *I am an asset. Going forward, I will list out times when I have succeeded and accomplished what I have set out to do, in order to remind myself of my value.*
>
> *I am worthy. Going forward, I will acknowledge that I deserve to be in any room I walk into as much as anyone else.*

If you want to fully own your narrative, you first have to take it back internally and understand where it came from. But it's not easy. And don't be discouraged if it takes a bit of time. It may be an ongoing process as you move through different chapters and circumstances in your career. The internalized bias and limiting beliefs may continue to pop up as you move along this path of self-discovery and empowerment.

But now that you're waking up to this, you'll be able to call it out in real time when the feelings reemerge, and you'll be ready to face the next step in the journey, and the one after that, until one day you'll find that you have effectively, like the badass you are, changed the old narrative. Then you can start to focus on being able to communicate that to others and finding your voice through all the bias fog that may be surrounding your environment—that's the next step in our journey that we'll explore. Ultimately, though, it's all about turning the page and continuing to discover you, to strengthen you. Once you identify what's been happening within you and do the internal work, the outer shift will begin, and you can really start stepping into your power.

4

Take the Damn Risk

When was the last time you took a career risk? Like hearing of an opportunity or catching a quick lead and hopping on it? Whether that lead was just a bolt of inspiration to take on a new project, a job opportunity, or something else, have you been able to get proactive and harness the confidence to do something about it? If not, what stopped you? There are a number of things that can keep us stagnant and stuck in our tracks. Sometimes it's uncertainty and doubt: *I don't know if I have what it takes.* Other times it just feels like too much of a risk: *What if I waste time doing something that doesn't pay off?* But often it really comes down to fear: *Am I really ready? Qualified? Good enough for this?*

To start breaking down our roadblocks to success, let's dig deep on what's stopping us in the first place. Whether these emotions are provoked by our ruminations on our own self-worth or stirred up by our environment, it can lead us to self-alienate or segregate ourselves from the spaces and people we need to be to get ahead. We take our names out of the hat even before we give ourselves a chance to prove our worth to others. One of the greatest impediments to our chance of success is inaction.

As women of color, immigrants, and children of immigrants, we should think about our relationship with rules. Take for example how we might view a list of job requirements for a new job. Would you apply to it if you met most requirements? Or would you see them set in stone, only applying if you met them to a T? Then there's the understanding of how bias and stereotypes play out in hiring processes and decision-making for new job opportunities. We've all experienced the fear of not knowing if it's worth applying to a given position, whether our efforts will go anywhere, and whether we will experience bias. While we know the millions of ways an opportunity could end up playing out if left in the hands of someone else and their preconceived notions, it's worth noting the part we can control: our own relationship with risk and to what extent limiting beliefs play a role in our perception of that risk. We also have to be clear on the root of some of our hesitancies in going for opportunities that have the potential to take our career to the next level in the first place.

Even if we don't find ourselves with fully fleshed-out opportunities at work yet, we have the ability to find and create them in unexpected places and turn an obstacle into our next shot at success. Because no one is going to take our hand and show us step by step how to develop our careers. That's a vision we need to create for ourselves. We've got to learn how to combat any noise from others, feel worthy, and get into action to get ahead.

Think about a current roadblock you're up against, whatever you feel is keeping you stagnant. What's stopping you from taking that next step? What is fueling the idea that this is a risk you're up against? Are you sitting in a pool of incessant what-if thoughts, uncertainty, and fear of the unknown? I know how stunting and debilitating that endless loop can be. So let's try to counteract it. Start by recalling and emotionally reconnecting to a moment in your life when you defied all odds and went after an opportunity without allowing your churning mind to hold you back or get in your way. What feelings can you remember in the moment when you conquered that opportunity? Channel that!

Before I got my foot in the door at NBCUniversal, as someone who just wanted a normal on-the-books job, I really had no idea how exactly I'd go about developing the whole career thing. In fact, I was all over the place. But I did come to the realization that I wanted to find a way to work in media so I could help make a difference. I wanted to amplify the voices of marginalized people so more of us could feel seen and heard, and help create and shape how our stories were told. As an undocumented twenty-something with zero experience or connections in the industry, that was a tall order. There was a part of me that obsessively fantasized about a time and place without the legal restrictions I had in front of me. I dreamed of living in New York City, working for a big media company, and being in a decision-making role where I had the power to better represent and give voice to people of marginalized communities. But how?

While in college in Ohio, I'd find myself going from restaurant job to housecleaning gig, scrubbing tables and toilets to pay my tuition while daydreaming about where I wanted to be professionally after graduation. I didn't want to settle for doing odd jobs like these all my life.

We've worked too hard to think that we don't deserve it all. No matter where you are in your career, whether you're just starting out or well into it, chances are you're reading this book because you've already used sweat and elbow grease, made sacrifices and maybe shed tears, all in the name of success and accomplishment. So don't stop now. Face those intrinsic fears and emerging feelings of self-doubt, and power through toward what you *really* want in your career and life.

At the time, when I made a commitment to myself to work toward a career that mattered to *me*, I was about to graduate with no professional future and no papers, just a ton of money invested in a diploma that I didn't know if I would be able to use. *What the hell do I have to lose?* I remember thinking when I started flooding New York's unpaid internship scene with applications, sending cover letters and résumés to any and all opportunities I could get my hands on. I wasn't wearing a powerful superwoman cape—quite the opposite. I was just out there pushing through feelings of doubt and fear that I couldn't have what I wanted. I'd spend night after night staying up late, obsessively perfecting my résumé: *Garamond or Times New Roman? Left indent at 0.5 or 1.5?* I was ready to dive headfirst into any opportunity to move to and work in New York City.

Instead of trying to claim the whole apple orchard, I started by focusing on getting myself in a space where I could start to plant apple seeds. I was scared and stressed, and I didn't feel that great about my chances, but I kept chugging forward. I applied to marketing agencies, to unheard-of startups I dug up from the internet, even boutique jewelry companies. Basically anyone who needed an intern. I sent Hail Mary applications to media companies like MTV Networks. On the surface, many of these places didn't seem to relate to the media world I dreamed of reaching, but it would be on me to connect the dots later. I also didn't have a work permit, so if I heard back from one of these companies (and that felt like a big if), I knew I'd have to get creative about explaining that. But I'd figure it out as I went. I'd convinced myself that I just needed a way into the city of opportunity, where I could get the necessary exposure to the professional world that would get me one step closer to building my career.

The only thing I was confident about was the likelihood of hearing back from someone, *anyone*, if I played the numbers game. In a weird way, failure cultivated hope when I felt helpless. I figured that, statistically, the more nos or closed doors I got, the closer I would get to some type of yes, even if that meant coming in through a side door. I learned then the lesson I so fervently use now to travel down my path: your green light is just a few red and yellow stops away. Except mine felt like they were miles away, during rush hour, on the West Side of Manhattan, on a Monday. But remember, obstacles can turn into opportunities.

I was at the town's library doing my daily research on job listings when I heard my phone ring, looked down, and saw the 212 New York area code. I died momentarily, then answered the call, my fingers trembling. I took a deep breath and eased into the classic round of initial niceties and interview talk. This was it, and I was ready. And then came the clincher.

"We could actually see you at this time tomorrow. You're local, right?" said the hiring manager on the other end of the line. I held my breath as I pictured her skimming through the top of my résumé, reading the New York City address I had confirmed as my own: 116th and Broadway—an address I'd found on Google that seemed vaguely linked with Columbia University.

"Yes! Yes, I am," I lied, the sound of my self-assuredness catching me off guard.

"Good, we'll see you tomorrow," she said as she wrapped up the call and gave me the address of Bad Boy Entertainment, the company founded by music mogul Sean Combs, better known at the time as P. Diddy.

"Yes, I'll be there," I whispered through half breaths as I hung up and dropped my phone, dizzy with excitement, my hands shaking.

After the adrenaline of the phone-screening interview began to wane, I snapped back to my reality: I had just confirmed I would be at an in-person interview in New York City the next day when I was actually deep in Ohio!

I had assumed that a small entertainment agency offering unpaid internships beginning in two weeks' time would prioritize candidates who, aside from being qualified, were accessible, so I told a little white lie. I could hear the excuses the hiring managers would have used if they had known I was in Ohio: *She's too far. She'd need help finding housing. An unpaid internship in New York City would be too expensive for an out-of-stater.* I imagined them tossing out my résumé, coming up with their own preconceived notions about me. I had faced enough closed doors and bias to know that people usually jumped to conclusions based on their own ideas, and I didn't want to take any chances with my shot at this opportunity.

Panicked and in way over my head, I dived into problem-solving mode. It was an instinct that came naturally—finally, a benefit to my neurotic, type A, eldest-sibling personality! While trying to control the speed of my heart, which felt like it could explode any second, I had to remember that the thing I'd been hoping for had actually just happened. I was up against time, and I couldn't afford to blow it. I had to walk the walk and set aside any fear that would get in the way of my goal.

How in the heck would I get to Manhattan? I asked myself over and over again. Since I didn't have an ID or a car, getting on a plane or driving was out of the question. I went with my gut and scoured the internet for the first bus out. It had been that same gut reaction of fearlessness that pushed me to apply for and enroll in college despite not having a plan for how I was going to pay for it, let alone how I would graduate. It was the same feeling that always propelled me forward even when the path ahead was murky.

My mind was racing. *Will I make it on time? How do these long bus routes work anyway? What will I do when I get there? Is this . . . safe?*

A few nervous clicks later, I purchased my Greyhound bus ticket, called my mom, and word-vomited my plans for an unpaid internship in New York City.

"¿Un internship? ¿Qué es eso? New York? ¡No conocemos a nadie ahí!" she noted unhelpfully, aggravating my nerves even more. It would take months for her to understand exactly what an internship was and why I decided to turn my world upside down to go for it.

"Okay, Mom, can you just pick me up and take me to the bus station in Cincinnati?"

"Daniela, pero I'm three hours away, and my shift ends in three hours. I wouldn't be able to today, but... Wait, why are you—"

"Okay, gotta go, bye!"

There was no time for long-winded explanations. I needed to find a ride to the bus station, stat. With no time to waste, I called my only friend with a car on campus.

"I can't explain much but can you drop me off in Cincinnati? I'll give you money for gas, pretty please!"

"Sure, when?"

"In the next... hour or so."

And just like that, I was on my way to Cincinnati, Ohio, hoping I'd make it in time to catch the next bus out. I packed only the essentials in my purse, and identified a suitable interview outfit that I'd carry on a hanger. I knew I'd have to come back the same day since I couldn't afford a hotel, but I also couldn't show up to the interview with a huge bag of stuff like a weirdo.

Around three a.m., after riding down highways for what felt like forever, the bus from Ohio finally pulled into Philadelphia, where it was scheduled to unload overnight. I had to transfer to another bus, which wasn't due to leave for another few hours. Although it was the tail end of spring, the temperature dropped drastically that night—it was freezing! I'd decided to travel light to avoid raising any eyebrows by rolling up to an interview with a big bag of clothes (I was supposed to be local, after all), which meant there had been no room to pack extra layers.

Shivering and struggling to stay awake, I forced myself to thumb through data on the company's latest marketing projects and jot down a few outside-the-box ideas on branding in case those questions came my way. Between the pressure to prepare, my overall nerves about whether things would run smoothly enough with the buses to get me to the interview on time, and the sketchy older guy who kept looking over at me, sleep wasn't in the cards for me.

The truth is that I probably should have been a bit more concerned by the fact that I was only twenty years old, alone, and at a bus stop in the middle of the night in a city that was more than five hundred miles away from home. But I wasn't at all. Someone else may have dismissed it as a menial unpaid internship not worth risking your safety, time, and money for, but in my eyes, it was my golden ticket.

Meanwhile, my mom was terrified, and rightly so—I never told her that on my overnight bus ride back from New York, I woke up to the man next to me slyly brushing his hand against my chest. But she knew better than to try to stop me once I had made up my mind. So she resorted to the only thing she could do at the time: she set an alarm to wake herself up every two hours to check up on me in the middle of the night. The truth is that neither of us slept, but if there was anything my uphill battles had taught me, it was to think big while never losing focus on the small actions that could ultimately get me there.

This work opportunity, as far as I was concerned, had the potential to give me access to the professional blueprint I wanted, so no amount of intrinsic danger or risk would stop me from giving it a shot.

Eighteen hours later, I arrived, sleep-deprived, at Port Authority. I rushed to find the nearest bathroom, where I had just enough time to clean myself up, apply makeup, and change into my H&M pencil skirt and blouse (which, after I ran it under the sink and hand drier for ten minutes, managed to unravel itself from the wrinkles created on the trip).

A sea of cars flooded the street with loud honks, and the smell of exhaust fumes mixed with caramelized peanuts hit me as I stepped out of the Forty-Second Street bus station. Trying to navigate these unfamiliar streets, I whipped out the MapQuest directions I had printed, which guided me down Broadway into a skinny building nestled between a Serafina restaurant and a Starbucks.

Bad Boy Entertainment Worldwide

I read the thin gold letters on the awning and took an extra-deep breath, blinking twice to make sure I wasn't dreaming. The last twenty-four hours were a blur, a series of what felt like movie scenes strung together. Did I imagine sitting on the cold floor of a bus station in the middle of the night, alone? Getting to New York? Walking through Times Square? I could see the scenes in my head, but in all my haste, it didn't feel real...until now.

You've got this, Daniela, I said to myself. *Deep breaths.* That inner cheerleader that I had learned to depend on in moments of fear appeared, right when I needed her the most.

A young receptionist took my information, and I waited in the lobby for what seemed like hours, with nerves twisting my stomach into endless knots. My eyes kept going back to the TV in the corner of the room playing a video on loop: "CEO, founder of Bad Boy Entertainment, music mogul, tastemaker, trendsetter, icon...Puff Daddy, P. Diddy, Sean John, Sean Combs..."

Holy shit, I can't believe I'm here!

"Change your name, then change it again," Diddy said in the video.

I tried my best to keep my cool, which wasn't very easy for someone with very little experience of what "cool" looked like. My insides were jumping with giddiness. I had never seen a famous person in real life, and now I might have the chance to work for one?! *Note to self: Do not by any means bring up this uncool thought in the interview. Pull. Yourself. Together.*

Finally, someone escorted me to the interview a few floors up. My nerves subsided a bit as I looked around—a group of young professionals of diverse backgrounds busily zipped around the room. Having grown up as the only Latina in a predominantly white town, seeing faces of all shades put me at ease.

Greeting me for my interview was a tall, model-like Asian woman with impeccable style. I was immediately intimidated. We sat down in a conference room, where I started doing this weird curtsy thing with my legs in front of her, attempting to hide my $9.99 Payless black flats.

After about ten minutes of questions about my background, why I wanted to work as a marketing intern, and other general questions about the job, I assured her that no matter how small or big the job was, I'd be up for the task.

And then I fessed up, telling her the truth about the trip and that I hadn't just hopped off the subway but had taken an overnight bus in order to be there in person.

"You know, we could have done this via videoconference,"

she said, a bit taken aback at hearing me explain the long trek I had just endured.

"I wanted to make sure you knew I was serious about this opportunity."

It was true. I wanted to prove to them I was worth the hire. But in hindsight, I now understand that I was also reckoning with my own sense of inadequacy. Applying to this job felt out of my league, and so getting on the bus and strategizing my steps was a tangible way to build my own confidence and help ease my self-doubts.

Sometimes, when we meet with new, exciting opportunities and we feel insecure, our best bet is to look for ways to build trust with ourselves that we've got what it takes. Putting action behind our own inadequacies can sometimes be a formula for reverse engineering what seems like an insurmountable obstacle or scary challenge.

Up until my confession, the interviewer's questions had been bulleted my way with hastiness, almost as if she was expecting the content of my responses. There must have been dozens of others who sat in that same chair before I did, answering the same types of routine questions. It was clear she had work to get done, and this interview was one more thing she needed to check off her to-do list. I didn't take her abruptness personally; I was too excited to just be there.

But after I explained my trip, her tone changed. Her expression became softer, and she began to slow down and show genuine interest in learning more about me. She followed up with questions that implied I had now made it to the third round of interviews.

Third round?

I now had to put together a PowerPoint presentation on a branding idea to showcase my marketing competence. But I could do that via email—*whew*.

Once we were done, I walked myself out and waved goodbye to the doorman, who responded with a serendipitous "See you soon."

Whether that was routine or not, I took it as a sign.

As the sun hid behind the towering Midtown building, I made my way to Times Square to catch my bus back to Ohio. *If this works out, I'm going to find a way to see it through,* I thought amid the lights, the power, that emanated from Forty-Second Street. The chaos of honking horns, the sea of diverse people hastily walking somewhere, and the outright energy made me feel like anything was possible. I fell head over heels in love. This place, although very unfamiliar to me, made me feel strangely at home.

I'll be back, I told myself.

So far, my choices and options were limited to what my environment dictated. I had been stuck for so long, feeling defeated because I couldn't change my environment. But now, although I had not been accepted for the internship yet, I felt an odd sense of being in control, something I had rarely felt in the past. I wasn't in control of their ultimate decision about me, of course, but I did feel power over the narrative I had consciously created. I had a certain sense that I could offer my decision to make the trip there as tangible proof of who I was: disciplined, scrappy, self-assured. The reward outside whether I got the gig or not was a deeper understanding of trusting my gut.

On the bus back to Ohio, I was too high on adrenaline to sleep or think about anything else other than the interview earlier that day and my fantasy of moving to New York City that summer. This was a step, *the* step, that could give me the exposure to the professional world I wanted to enter. I was reeling with excitement that I'd taken it.

I had no guarantee this would work out, that it would pay off, or even that I could make use of this experience down the road. I had no paperwork to work at a real company that required proper identification, and if I did get this unpaid internship, I'd be more exposed legally. And how would I even afford to live in one of the most expensive cities in the world without financial support or networks? But I had to see this through. It was a full test of the size of my own self-trust—my knowledge that I was willing to follow through and take a risk without leaving anything on the table. When you realize that no one is going to come save you, extend their hand, or even offer counsel, you start thinking differently. I found power in knowing that it was up to me and only me to go for what I wanted, and that it could possibly, maybe, somehow work out, even when it felt like I was way out of my league. And, boy, was I out of my league.

But I was determined to fight for what I wanted, to create a space for myself, to make room for who I wanted to be—to battle my feelings of otherness and alienation, bury my sense of inadequacy, and keep going.

Many of us don't have the luxury to wait for perfect conditions in order to go after our goals and the type of lives we want for ourselves. If I had waited to have enough money, waited for someone to tell me what to do and how, waited for mentors, waited to see someone else do it first, waited to feel fully confident in what I was doing, chances are I wouldn't have gotten that job and I wouldn't be where I am today.

I was confident that I'd be able to follow through once I had the opportunity. The real lesson was acting on that confidence before I let myself ruminate on any what-ifs, fears, or potential biases I might encounter.

It is true that sometimes our weaknesses can be our strengths. In a way, my circumstances and undocumented status pushed me into a *What do I have to lose?* mentality and forced me to rely on other important traits, like self-trust and my worthiness. The world told people like me, *You are illegally taking up space*, but rather than let my environment dictate my life, I had to dig deep to emotionally, physically, and spiritually debunk that narrative and give myself a chance to chart a different path. It takes trial and error to leap before you know what's ahead, to go for that opportunity or job even if it's scary and allegedly out of reach for an "other." At the end of the day, our experiences, our circumstances, our lives have already taught us that no matter what is thrown our way, we can figure it out.

When I moved to New York and started the internship, I was scared shitless. Every move I made was a risk. In those offices, I felt vulnerable, and I did hear voices in my head saying:

Who do you think you are?

What makes you think you'll succeed?

What if this doesn't work out?

Do you really have what it takes?

But whatever feelings of inadequacy I had during my first

months on the job—and there were many, related to how I dressed, how I acted, and how much I knew—subsided when I realized how hard I had worked to get there. To get myself there. I didn't know going in that a byproduct of the whole ordeal of attempting to attain the internship would be something greater than monetary compensation: learning to trust myself. There is a deep sense of confidence you start cultivating when you knowingly put yourself in situations out of your comfort zone and navigate through them.

Perfectionism is a slow-eating monster chomping away at your dreams. It slows us down in so many ways. I was scrappy and eager without knowing what would come next. And although sometimes that meant being messy along the way without having a traditional path, it was who I was, and I started to embrace the beauty of it. Slowly, I began to develop a confidence that wavered less and less in the face of outside archetypes of success.

Confidence is like a muscle. You can make it stronger by seeking out chances to learn something new, putting yourself out there, and challenging yourself to go outside your comfort zone. Our level of confidence is not a fixed psychological state—it can be cultivated and strengthened by our actions. I still get self-conscious, second-guess myself, get nervous in groups of higher-ups, and so on, but what I rely on is an understanding of how important it is to put myself out there. To give myself a chance. The trust you have in yourself and the long-term effects of listening to your gut are priceless. But you have to give yourself a chance before you can expect anyone else in the world to do so.

Take Andrea, a junior public relations associate who got her foot in the door working for a high-profile, highly sought-after

PR exec in a major city. It was a position that she could only have dreamed of a couple of years earlier. As the only Latina in the office, she made an effort to cultivate relationships with up-and-coming brands catering to Latinas in the beauty space. She was eager to prove her worth to her boss and encourage more communication and partnerships with Latino-based brands. She was passionate about the importance of expanding inclusivity at her company and wasn't afraid to put her own experience as a Latina and her publicity prowess to work. But when it came time for the company to put time and dollars toward collaborating with the Latino brands she was pitching, nothing happened. To the mostly white senior teams, this Latino beauty space felt "smaller." After repeatedly bumping against this wall and not getting any traction with her efforts, she eventually stopped trying. She didn't come into this job feeling inadequate, but the workplace culture was slowly digging away at her.

Then, just before she began to seriously contemplate leaving the company, her higher-ups invited her to a meeting with a potential new client—a big brand name. *I never get invited to join these meetings,* she thought, hoping this was the next step she had been tirelessly working for in order to be taken more seriously. As the meeting unfolded, she quickly realized that this new client was working on a new product rollout aimed at Latina consumers and was seeking this company's "expertise" in the market. Great! This was her time to shine. Yet as the meeting dragged on, she spent the entire hour eagerly trying to chime in, only to be ignored. That's when it hit her: *I'm not here for my ideas. I'm here because I look like I fit the part.* She felt her voice didn't truly count. At the end of the day, this wasn't about giving Andrea a moment to step up in her role and gain more ownership of the expertise she had been advocating for months; it was about helping the agency win over the client by offering them a false idea of their own diversity. They didn't want to make it seem like it was just a bunch of white people trying to market to a demographic of women of color—but that was the straight truth. Andrea felt like she was just a prop to them.

Once it all began to sink in, she realized that if she remained there, she'd constantly be kept down at the low end of the hierarchy. Leaving a company with cachet felt risky, but she held on to a belief that anchored her more than the fear of the regret she'd feel about leaving; she deserved to work for a company that valued diversity and her unique ability to promote it. So she defied the inadequacy they made her feel in that office and created her own opportunity by founding a boutique PR agency exclusively representing Latinas and other people of color.

Whether you're like me, who got a job and carried the feeling of inadequacy in my mind based on my experiences growing up, or like Andrea, who had the feeling of inadequacy imposed on her by her colleagues, you don't have to accept it. You can fight it in your own way. You don't necessarily have to quit your job or jump on a bus and travel hundreds of miles to land an opportunity like Andrea and I did—sometimes, in order to remove these inner and outer obstacles and build your success, the first thing you need to do is become your own best cheerleader.

Reaching our goals starts with setting up an action-driven process, which ultimately helps redefine how we see risk and our relationship with fear. Here are four pillars to come back to when you're second-guessing yourself while assessing a career or work move.

1. **Break down the challenge.**

What's the issue at stake? Mine was that I didn't have a clear opening on how to build my career, both because I was undocumented and because I didn't have any networks or mentors.

What can you do to change it? Career-building opportunities started to open up when I began getting comfortable with putting myself out there, *consistently*, for opportunities I felt could be turning points in my career. Get comfortable putting yourself out there. Raise your hand in that meeting, take initiative, say the thing that no one is saying but that you feel is important, ask for more because that's what you know you deserve. This will reframe how you view risk. *What's the worst that can happen?* Losing out on an opportunity of greater success and fulfillment by not going for it.

2. **Trust that voice that pushes you toward the unconventional.**

When your current situation seems so uncertain and tough to handle or plan, lean into the power of creative thinking. You have control of what your future looks like, so use your own building blocks instead of trying to fit into a linear path of success. If you listen to your gut and do away with the idea that there must be a planned-out roadmap or guidebook that tells you how you can succeed, you'll give yourself more access to your goals than any other person could provide.

My big issue, in addition to being undocumented, was that I didn't have the right experience for a career in media—but what is the "right" experience anyway? When I started thinking outside the box about media opportunities and wasn't so fixated on being the "perfect" candidate, I found my footing, and then trusted myself on how I'd use that experience at Bad Boy to connect the dots of my experience and gain the access I needed to develop a full-blown career in media.

3. Get out of your own way.

Start paying attention to just how much mental energy you spend on negative thoughts about what you *don't* want instead of using that energy to plan out the actions you *do* want to take to develop your career. Get out of your own way. Think of the steps you need to take, even the small ones that can get you out of your head and into the *doing* territory. The best way to break the inertia is to keep going, no matter how small the effort toward your goal is. Repurposing our thoughts of doubt toward creating small solutions has a cumulative effect.

Days into my internship at Bad Boy, after one too many stomachaches from one-dollar slices of New York pizza, I realized that I needed to find any and all cash-paying jobs I could get my hands on to support this unpaid opportunity. I had zero income, and I hadn't actually graduated yet; I still had an upcoming semester of school left to pay for. But my years of working in restaurants, selling Mary Kay products, and dealing with unknowns gave me the training wheels I needed. I was ready to hustle and do whatever it took to make the unpaid internship work and support myself.

First, I hit Restaurant Row, a section of Forty-Sixth Street near the theater district overflowing with restaurants. I walked into each and every one, résumé in hand, and asked to speak to the manager in order to pitch myself for any on-the-spot opportunities. No one was hiring. Reminding myself, *It's a numbers game*, I took the hit and kept going. Craigslist and babysitting websites were up next. After applying for everything I could find, I scored side gigs as a babysitter, a pet sitter, and a dog walker by day, all of which I squeezed in during my lunch breaks or after I clocked out. And twice a week, I worked at a bar and as a club promoter by night.

One day I was in a new city with zero connections, and in a matter of weeks I was in the center of New York life, jumping from one job to the next, moving through the city like I'd been living there for years. Sure, I was in over my head, but it was so worth it. It was my chance to reverse engineer my way to my bigger career goals. I'm not advising you to burn yourself out or become a workaholic; I was in my early twenties at the time and still had the energy to overwork myself. But the point is for you to start thinking beyond negative self-talk like *This sounds impossible; I can't; No one else has done it this way*. Turn your what-ifs into why-nots and use your energy on small actions that will help you achieve your bigger goal. Small actions can lead to big results.

4. Remove the fear from the yes.

Sometimes the thought of receiving a yes can be scarier than receiving a no. Sometimes we make a million excuses for why things can't happen for us, because it feels safer. Safe is comfortable, and who wants to be uncomfortable? A yes might be uncharted territory. Yes often means change, which requires learning new ways of navigating the world or holding power we might not feel ready to hold.

While Andrea might not have necessarily wanted to up and leave her company, she had to face reality: *Do I fear quitting my job and dealing with all the things that come with starting my own company, like being in charge of my own salary and success?* Because as exciting as being your own boss may sound, she had to contend with a lot of responsibility and unknowns to make it possible. Shifting her course and building her own opportunity eventually brought her the success she wanted, but it required her to make changes that were often difficult.

All facets of opportunity and success have consequences—more responsibility, more authority, and sometimes, more haters. At the core, there is a vulnerability we have to get comfortable with. It will take time to handle your newfound success. New feelings of doubt will likely crop up, or you may even feel a rush of guilt for getting what you want, but this is all part of the change we want to see for ourselves. It's our chance to align that change with our potential. We have to welcome the change that may come with our increased success and trust ourselves to find a way to support our achievements.

When I landed that first internship, I celebrated—then quickly realized that ahead of me lay the task of having to move to one of the most expensive cities in the world *and* put myself at legal risk in a work setting because I was undocumented. In some ways, hearing that yes was terrifying, because it meant I would have to deal with a bunch of other unknowns. But realizing that my terror was grounded in the fear of actually achieving what

I wanted made it more empowering. I was getting closer to my purpose, even if I didn't have it all figured out yet.

If you feel it's time for you to step into action toward your work and career goals, just know that it will require both micro- and macro-level risks. You may find you will have to go beyond what you even thought you were capable of—and maybe what others thought you were capable of as well. But if you're willing to put in the work, you'll start to see opportunities in places you didn't think existed. You are good enough. You do deserve it. You probably don't know it all, but that isn't a bad thing. You'll learn. It's just important to know that you don't need permission to start creating the life and career you want now.

5

Duality Is Your Superpower

'll never forget my first day of basketball training back in sixth grade. I was twelve years old, I had just started middle school in the United States, and it was the first time I had ever stepped foot on a basketball court. Our coach was a student's parent, and very much a fan of the tough love approach. As we filed in for our first practice, he gave us orders to do laps around the gym. Laps? The only sport I had done in Chile was rhythmic gymnastics, which for us basically just meant waving long, flowy ribbons into different shapes. Most of our practices consisted of stretching and working on a synchronized routine with our ribbons, which would inevitably end up in messy knots halfway through our end-of-the-year recital. So yes, laps were something foreign to me—literally.

I also didn't get the memo on proper athletic wear for such a sport as basketball. The day before, I'd gone to Kmart and bought what I thought would be a sensible option: a cute baby-blue-and-white skort and a matching tank top with a collared neck. *¡Qué lindo!* I remember thinking. You can imagine the head-to-toe stares I got from the girls on the team, who donned loose-fitting shorts and old sport camps tees. Being "the foreign girl" was probably explanation enough of my outfit.

Shouldn't we all get in a circle and introduce ourselves? I thought. *Share fun facts or something?* Not with this group. Most of them already knew each other from years of rotating on and off the team and the many summers spent at "all-star camps." I didn't fully understand the concept of spending a whole summer away at a camp playing basketball indoors. When pamphlets were distributed at the end of the season, I quickly realized it wasn't just basketball camps—it was volleyball, soccer, softball, cheerleading, and so on. All I could think was, *How do these people afford it?* But sports were a big part of their world, often at the insistence of their parents, and given that most had been playing since they were young, they were well conditioned when it came to practice and training.

I, on the other hand, was clueless, to say the least. *This is what death probably feels like,* I thought on that first day, several laps into our warm-up exercises. My heart felt like it was going to explode, but I kept going.

The sports-centeredness of my new home, especially for young women, was unfamiliar to me. Eventually, even though I was never all that athletic—like, at all—I couldn't get enough of it. And I still managed to end the seasons with awards like "Best Team Spirit" or "Most Improved." (LOL.) After the third year of getting "Most Improved," I realized that what kept me coming back for more was the competition, the sportsmanship, the push for self-improvement and success, and the friendships.

These opportunities really made the difference between me sulking at home over factors that put me at a disadvantage—like not feeling a real sense of belonging in this new middle- to upper-class school environment—and me focusing my energy in the right place to reach my full potential. And I chose the latter, even though early on I knew I would have to constantly compensate for my otherness. But I loved the rewards the environment brought: recognition, praise, respect, wins, and friends. In some ways, it was a metaphor for what I loved about this country and the unlimited opportunities it promised. It was a whole new environment where I could craft an entirely different identity.

My experience is, in some ways, an exaggerated version of what many people go through when there's a cultural learning curve in assimilating. Social cues on how to be included and find belonging are part of how we engage with the world, how we seek to be seen and heard by others. Part of navigating any workplace is getting good at reading the cues around us and figuring out how to best respond to them. From email and Zoom etiquette, to coworker power dynamics, to the morning coffee rush in the tiny staff kitchen, to handling office politics and group projects, you need some kind of self-awareness on how to position yourself.

Social cues in any situation can be frustrating and confusing, but this is especially true in work settings. The vibe says to be ambitious...but not *too* ambitious. Eager...but not *too* eager. Trying to strike the perfect balance to blend in requires interpreting a myriad of mixed messages about who you need to be—and not be—to succeed. In certain workplaces, it can be straightforward; there's a real company culture in place. Other times, it's not so simple. On top of that, the pandemic made the idea of work culture even muddier. It's nearly impossible to create an understanding of a company's culture through a screen. Whether it's what you're allowed to say, who you're allowed to say it to, or another issue entirely, in most jobs we have to strategically adjust to our work environments and repeatedly monitor ourselves to try to avoid causing dissonance or discomfort along the way.

The problem is, if the environment is ambiguous, this can drive you nutty or make you ultra self-aware in a toxic way. But often we play along anyway, to fit in or to be seen in the same light as others so we can gain access and equal opportunity. Ultimately, in work spaces, we are all in some crosscurrent of identities and lived experiences, influenced by the people and environments around us, enabling us as others to become chameleons. This is our superpower. It allows us to survive in certain spaces. And by doing so, we learn to fit in and function in different worlds.

While doing the internship with Bad Boy Entertainment, I also heard back from Viacom. They were looking for an intern at MTV's advertising sales department—a less glamorous, but quite important, part of the media business. I negotiated doing both part-time: Bad Boy three days a week and Viacom two. I was working with one company that was predominantly staffed by people of color and another that was predominantly white. All I wanted was to fit into both.

At Bad Boy, I was surrounded by the most boss women I've ever met: larger-than-life marketing executives who were mostly Black women, tall, with Barbie-like looks, dressed to the nines in brand-name outfits and stilettos. They were sharp, serious, deeply hardworking women, and they had that instant executive authority with a direct demeanor that didn't mince words—they were exactly who I wanted to be like and learn from. So I set out to assimilate into this new environment.

I realized the easiest first step to blending in would be to have the right wardrobe. During my first week, I left work one day and headed straight to a discount store to buy a knockoff designer dress to better mimic the office's general stylishness. But the joke was on me, because I literally knew no designer names outside of what was sold in my hometown's very sparse selection at Macy's. Then I slipped into Aldo, where I chose the highest and thinnest pair of heels I could find. *There. Now I look like them,* I thought proudly.

The next morning, when one of the execs called me over to give me my task for the day, I sashayed my way over to her, barely keeping my balance in those ridiculously high four-inch heels, nonetheless excited to show off this new and improved, can-hang-in-a-big-city me. No way I was going to give off small-town, fish-out-of-water vibes. Surely, she'd say something about how fashion-forward I looked—ha, so I hoped.

Instead, when I walked into her office, she gave me an up-and-down once-over, eyebrows raised and lips pursed. "I know you're trying to do your 'thing,' but right now I need you to go upstairs and assemble the swag closet," she said, dismissing my embarrassing effort to be chic with a bless-your-heart smirk.

I was mortified! Obviously. I quickly learned that not all workplace culture is one-size-fits-all—that was the last time I attempted to dress for a job that I didn't have or couldn't do my job in. My intentions were good, but that clothing wasn't practical for someone just starting out in the office whose main tasks were cleaning and organizing closets of swag in an attic, delivering products, handling numerous Starbucks runs, and doing other random errands all day.

Although it's a squirmy story (that I can now laugh at), it does show the lengths we'll go to follow perceived rules of engagement at work, some of which we pick up inadvertently. *I don't just have to work for them, I have to* become *them*—or so I thought.

Although the stilettos may seem like an inconsequential example, they were a microcosm of how I'd operated all my life. There was a part of me that had always believed I had to change to fit my environment, that in any given situation, I had to look for hidden rules to follow. I'd spend tons of energy making assumptions about what everyone was thinking and then change the way I talked, dressed, and engaged in order to make them feel I was like them. This default tendency that had been present most of my life made my relationship with rules quite different from most other people's. I was a professional shape-shifter, constantly trying to fit in by following rules, all in the name of "inclusion."

Inclusion is a concept you tell yourself is needed in order to belong to spaces where you don't feel you naturally fit in. Growing up undocumented, I was consistently aware of my impression on others and often changed parts of myself to blend in. I was what is called a "high self-monitoring" person, meaning that I was sensitive to social and situational cues. I learned to control my self-expression and the way I carried myself so I could fit a certain mold I thought would be acceptable to others.

It proved to be a crucial survival skill in my small town, and I often recruited my family to participate in my antics. I convinced them that "blending in" was necessary and beneficial. I was always on edge, feeling I needed to fend off stereotypes or whispers of suspicion around my family's immigration status. The rules of inclusion felt safe and steady—they were the tools I used to control the chaos and uncertainty that came with being the eldest of five siblings and battling our housing and financial insecurities. I not only followed the rules, but I also took on the role of rule enforcer, demanding my siblings be enrolled in sports (even if they didn't like it), giving them unsolicited advice on their wardrobe to fit in with everyone else, and a bevy of other rules I had conjured to make sure they were starting off life in the United States on the right foot. I was a terror of a big sister.

But a lot of my issues had to do with minimizing any opportunity for others to notice the difference between *them* and *us*. I knew how immigrants were viewed in my town, and I didn't want to buy into the stereotype that led people in my community to be dismissive or look down on us. I'd be damned if I got fewer opportunities or was looked at differently just because of the gaps between our backgrounds. If I could just figure out the rules of belonging and play along with what everyone else was doing, I'd be one step closer to being on an equal playing field with my peers. I could chameleon my way toward my goals. And for a while, it worked.

I charged forward, working to fit into boxes everywhere I could. *Boxes are safe. Safe is good,* I told myself. I'd groomed myself to belong in spaces that felt out of my reach by using any cues I could find as my parameters. I did this in both my personal and my professional life, whether in the Midwest or in Manhattan—adjusting my wardrobe, learning the lingo, changing my demeanor to fit everyone else's, following their same cadence, adopting their slang, whatever was needed. It became second nature. I felt a responsibility to find a way to be relatable to others. I needed to manufacture a way for them to understand and accept me. I calculated my tone and demeanor consistently, and that quickly became my MO in so many other areas of my life. I knew what caused dissonance, became cognizant of other people's stereotypes or the limits on their expectations of me, and was able to shift into a version of myself that contradicted their notions of who I was as a Latina and an immigrant. I focused on finding a way to become palatable to them at the expense of feeling comfortable in my own skin.

I know you may have experienced the same, adjusting your accent to make the people around you feel more at ease, or adjusting your hair, jewelry, or outfits to fit the bill at work so they don't see you as too Asian, too Black, too Latino, etc. It took years for me to be comfortable wearing hoop earrings at work at my corporate job, because even as a proud Latina, I felt like it was *too* Latina-looking. (Lord, the internalized bias ran deep.) I did all of this and more so that I wasn't pigeonholed by my ethnicity instead of being valued for what I brought to the table.

Sticking to rules was my way of staying safe as I lived life undocumented, and I know you may be able to relate. We learn what to do and not do, what to say, how to say it, when not to say anything, and a multitude of other covering behaviors, because it feels like a protective shield.

In my case, being an undocumented immigrant comes with a multitude of implicit rules we need to follow as a way to "safely" stay in the shadows. We condition ourselves to respond on the spot, without a hint of hesitation, when someone asks about our status. We avoid situations where our IDs could be requested, like flying on a plane or driving a car—and if we are driving, we avoid certain intersections, take the back roads, and so on. We try not to bring too much attention to ourselves and our backgrounds. And, in some instances, we learn that in order to get certain educational opportunities (like applying to college), we must lie about how we got here. We avoid traps at all costs. So, ironically, I was living a life where my undocumented status effectively made me break the rules I so desperately yearned to follow. And it weighed on me.

Who we are, the circumstances we find ourselves in, what is required of us, and the limits we're up against as "others" can easily make us feel misaligned with society's rules, even those that are unsaid but still observed. A member of the LGBTQ community in a conservative area; a Black student at a majority-white Ivy League school; a hijab-wearing woman in STEM who struggles to be taken seriously among her male counterparts. The others are those who have to navigate these perceived misalignments and constantly monitor ourselves to get to where we want to be, compromising our own sense of authenticity in the process. But we power through all in the name of inclusion.

That's exactly what I did, until June 15, 2012…the biggest before-and-after day and ultimate moment of inclusion in my life.

I had just come back from my lunch break and was settling in to wrap up my tasks for the day at the Bad Boy offices when my phone lit up. Turn on the TV now, said a text from my mom. There were no televisions in our office, so I ran out to the deli a few doors down, and there, in the tiny corner television, I saw President Obama delivering an address from the White House Rose Garden.

"This morning," he said, "Secretary Napolitano announced new actions my administration will take to mend our nation's immigration policy."

He was referring to the almost one million undocumented students and young people who had been brought here, like me, as kids. The adrenaline rush hit me like a tsunami.

"These are young people who study in our schools, they play in our neighborhoods, they're friends with our kids, they pledge allegiance to our flag."

My throat tightened with overwhelming emotion.

"They are Americans in their heart, in their minds, in every single way but one: on paper," declared President Obama.

I suddenly forgot I was surrounded by strangers and immediately felt the urge to hug all ten patrons in the deli that day. I was totally unhinged with happiness. I eagerly glanced around, looking to make eye contact with someone who I could revel in the good news with, but they just ordered their subs and afternoon pick-me-ups like on any other day, completely unaware of how the news on TV was about to change my life. A waterfall of tears gushed down my cheeks. Euphoria, relief, joy, and gratitude shot up and down every cell in my body. I could not contain my joy.

President Obama went on. "Over the next few months, eligible individuals who do not present a risk to national security or public safety will be able to request temporary relief from deportation proceedings and apply for work authorization."

I can't write about this moment without getting full-body chills. It changed everything.

Up until that moment, I had no idea that this announcement to give a reprieve to people in my situation—one that I wasn't expecting and couldn't have foreseen—would carry such colossal meaning in my life. DACA (Deferred Action for Childhood Arrivals) was an executive action that would stop the United States from deporting young undocumented immigrants who entered the country as children if they met certain criteria. Those requirements included a thorough background check, having been in the United States before age sixteen, and currently being under the age of thirty. Eligible applicants must have been living here for at least five years and should be either in school, a high school graduate, or a military veteran in good standing, and have no prior criminal record. Check, check, check—I met all the benchmarks. And not only did it offer protection from deportation, but it would also allow for a work permit and other essential government paperwork I lacked, which had been the cause of so many doors glued shut on my path.

I was not alone. We were almost one million strong in the United States. Living in the shadows in Ohio, I had little perspective on how many others there were like me. It's not something that I felt comfortable sharing, so up until then, I had resorted to scouring online message boards like United We Dream, where other undocumented people would write in their legal queries, concerns, and fears, and we'd band together anonymously, trying to answer each other's questions and provide support for one another from our own lonely internet corners.

In 2001, the Development, Relief, and Education for Alien Minors (DREAM) Act was introduced to Congress—hence why some of us are called "Dreamers"—but it was never passed. The executive action the president resorted to that day was a last-ditch effort to help young people like me after the legislative branch failed to act. It was over a decade in the making, but it was not just a decision that originated within the White House. It was the result of the relentless and persistent work of hundreds of thousands of activists, grassroots programs, immigration advocates, and Dreamers who were undocumented and unafraid to come out of the shadows. Many of them didn't even qualify for the DACA program as it was written, because, by the time it actually went into effect, they wouldn't meet the age requirements. But nevertheless, they persisted, and DACA became what I needed to finally feel like I belonged. I could now apply for paid work and actually make a career for myself.

And I ran with it. I continued to work hard to be a "model minority"—the hardworking immigrant whose goodness rests on their productivity and their academic and professional efforts. That's what I was conditioned to understand was good and necessary, how I could prove to others I deserved to be here in this country. It became a way of subconsciously finding validation in tethering my value to the rules of inclusion. Work hard, put your head down, show others your value through your accomplishments. Show you're worthy of belonging. Aside from the fact that this approach perpetuates a bias that deems minorities "good" if they achieve it and "bad" if they have trouble achieving it, I realized it also said something about me that I thought being a "good" minority was defined by how well I felt I had assimilated to white culture. As if there were a monopoly on hard work. I didn't realize then that it would come with a cost to my identity.

I wore the forever-grateful model-minority immigrant identity on my forehead. And without really knowing it, I was walking on eggshells of my own making in most of my interactions during

those early years in my career, as I moved from Bad Boy Entertainment and Viacom to NBCUniversal, and then, at MSNBC,
eventually becoming a producer for *Morning Joe*. The moments of
doubt came up in subtle ways. As a new producer at MSNBC, I
found myself waiting to be instructed on which guests to pursue
for different news stories instead of proactively pitching and advocating for the ones I thought would be a good fit. I told myself I
was too junior, hiding behind the safety of following implicit rules.
But I felt stuck in a role of inferiority, often looking to my superiors
for my next move, calculating when it was okay to speak. Sure, it's
great to know how to read the room and understand what others
need, but when we're on autopilot reacting to what others expect of
us in the name of being the model minority, and we make a habit
of expressing ourselves solely based on what we think others want
to hear, the fabric of our uniqueness begins to unravel.

This conditioning makes it easier to feel our race, our gender,
our socioeconomic status, and we think that *we* are the ones who
need to change. Our undoing is often a product of survival. In
order to survive, we misclassify our differences as liabilities. What
should be seen as an advantage or a unique perspective is instead
seen as a burden. It doesn't help in our work environments that
we're already coming to the table with lived experiences that have
caused us to feel dismissed or not good enough because of who
we are and where we come from. These experiences stay with us.
Our minds, bodies, and souls remember the knots in our stom-
achs or our rapid heartbeats during the times we were on the
receiving end of discrimination, or even just the times we were
singled out as not quite fitting in, not belonging.

Of course, as we move along in our careers, when these lived experiences creep up again in a new form, we start to feel constrained, stuck. We hold off and clamp down on our dimensions and layers even tighter, and we repress and disguise who we are even more. Next thing we know, all the energy that we should be using to focus on work that aids in our advancement is instead being used to change something about ourselves. Instead of utilizing our differences as a strength, we've become so used to monitoring ourselves that it doesn't come easily to us to utilize our differences at work. As a result, many of us no longer even know how to openly express who we are effectively.

Your ability to show up with authority and confidence at work won't have a chance to develop if you're constantly constraining and checking yourself, or staying in your lane so as not to ruffle any feathers. Many times, as I sat in meetings and watched my colleagues and bosses ping-pong ideas in front of me, I quietly waited for the perfect moment to add my two cents, spending precious minutes calculating how I could deliver my idea in a perfectly wrapped package. But many times the moment never materialized. Meeting after meeting, I missed out on opportunities to show my value.

The truth is, no one is thinking about you as much as you are. No one can help you flourish and excel but you. You can have a thousand mentors, but you're still the one who has to take action. Being constantly aware of what others are thinking of us and how we're being perceived, instead of focusing on ourselves and the work at hand, can take up time and energy.

Throughout my life as an adolescent and teen, I had trouble separating my circumstances from my identity. I was falling prey to the narratives about my otherness that I believed others had.

Hell, I was still trying to define my identity to myself. Years of being uncomfortable in my skin made it hard to really lean into who I was and what I had to offer the world.

It wasn't until college that I longed to get back to the Latino roots I had perhaps unknowingly played down in order to fit into a predominantly white small town. As a newly independent adult, I found myself wanting to lean into my own unique voice and play up my Latinidad. Feeling more Latina—perhaps in contrast to the whiteness around me—I started to allow myself to also feel proud as a chilena who had a different experience from my peers. I finally understood the power of my own cultural duality. The added advantage of being different.

Then, by the time I was deep in my first year in New York, settled into my job, I started realizing little things I hadn't noticed before, like the way I also felt I had to *strive* for everything, from money to fitting in. The stakes felt high, all the time. I was full of awareness of how I grew up socioeconomically disadvantaged, perhaps not going to schools as prestigious as those my colleagues had gone to, not feeling as book smart as everyone around me. I was always comparing myself to others, whether it was because of my legal status, my socioeconomic background, or my culture. I had gotten in a destructive habit of rushing to judge myself. I struggled to pinpoint why I couldn't embrace all these different aspects of myself without having the urge to compare myself to others or make myself feel less than. There was little softness or ease to ground myself in. I was always bracing myself for the next new challenge, feeling like I had to prove myself, still reckoning with my own identity.

This hyperawareness manifested in physical ways, too. I began to notice that my shoulders were always tense; I speed-walked

everywhere with an ever-present sense of being late. I was jug-
gling too much and moving a mile a minute. I was consumed by
the pressure and anxiety that came with knowing that making
one wrong move could lead me to lose it all.

Even after receiving DACA, I was still psychologically conditioned to stay in survival mode. I was used to the fight-or-flight
mode that came to be part of my identity living in the shadows.
This quest to accomplish and overcome was my way of trying to
find belonging in this country. It was a constant race to keep my
identity in check, to be the model minority and good worker in
every room I entered.

Splitting our identity into several parts is what W. E. B. Du
Bois called "double consciousness." He was referring specifically to
the Black experience and the perils of dual identity for Black people
shortly after emancipation. Yet this still rings true today for people
of color, undocumented immigrants, and people in many marginalized communities—members of society who must move through
the world with a thick veil over who they are to preempt the inevitable consequences of discrimination. It's a duality that pushes us to
constantly walk the line between being what others expect us to be
and allowing ourselves to be who we really are, leaving a huge question mark on our individual identity. When we repress part of who
we are, we ultimately close ourselves off to ourselves.

Reckoning with our personal duality can be confusing and
hard. It requires us to acknowledge what parts of ourselves we've
given away to go under the radar, be accepted, find a way to be
included in white culture.

In a conversation I had with author and Princeton professor Eddie Glaude, he reminded me that through our double

consciousness comes second sight: an ability to understand the white world better because of the expanded awareness that allows us to navigate two different worlds. It deepens our understanding racially and culturally, and there is a lot of power in the awareness of knowing how to maneuver our way around two worlds. The duality of who we are and how we move through the world is actually an advantage in the workplace, and it's where we must realize our power. Although this duality may have been hard to master, we have the special ability to create a closer and deeper relationship with ourselves and with the world. We experience this double consciousness in the ways we feel limited but also in the benefits of our heightened perception.

If we look at the layers of ourselves, we'll see we have twice as much to offer, and that should fuel the confidence and strength we bring to each room we enter. Our duality is our superpower. But when we constantly outsource for acceptance or to belong, we are masking key parts of who we really are.

In *The Gifts of Imperfection*, Brené Brown writes, "Fitting in is about assessing a situation and becoming who you need to be to be accepted. Belonging, on the other hand, doesn't require us to *change* who we are; it requires us to *be* who we are." We must understand that fitting in and belonging are not interchangeable. You'll never fully feel like you belong in certain environments if you're driven by a need to fit in. Fitting in requires hiding and shielding parts of who you are. Eventually it can take on the ills of the double consciousness Du Bois wrote about. We find ourselves muted, shrunk, and further away from being our most authentic, effective selves.

How we see ourselves and our duality can have a direct effect on how we show up at work. Tori, an Asian American woman

from Connecticut, told me about the time a white female colleague whom she didn't know that well approached her in a rush
and exclaimed, "Tori, this is Andrew. He's learning Chinese. You
speak Chinese, don't you?" Another time her boss asked if Tori
could help her daughter with her paper on Chinese history. If her
colleagues had taken the time to get to know her, they would've
known that Tori spoke Mandarin, not Cantonese, which was
what Andrew was learning. And as for Chinese history, the truth
was that she had only recently begun to take an interest in any
kind of history, having been a communications major in school.
Though she recognized these work experiences as microaggressions, they also triggered issues with her sense of identity at work
that she began to carry around.

Tori spent her formative years trying to downplay her ethnicity and simply blend in. To her, her otherness followed her
everywhere, from the catcalls on her way home from school by
gross old men fetishizing Asian girls to strangers yelling, "Ni
hao!" Even within her family she felt like an outcast, because
she preferred speaking English instead of Chinese. Throughout
her childhood, she spent a lot of energy minimizing and even
feeling ashamed of her roots, and it was something she had still
never quite dealt with until she came into her professional life.
Back in school, she avoided hanging out with other Asian people, convincing herself she had nothing in common with them,
fearing she'd be labeled "fresh off the boat" if she interacted too
much with them. As much as she aspired to release herself from
the myriad of stereotypes assigned to her simply because she was
Asian, she definitely didn't feel like being approached at work
with everyone's questions about China.

"I'm slow when I speak Chinese," she'd joke. Although she actually spoke and wrote fluent Chinese, she did not want to appear *too* foreign in her mostly white surroundings. Her entire life felt like she'd been fighting to be seen as Tori and not "the Asian." She was angry and ashamed of spending so many years trying to bury that part of her. Reckoning with her identity and ridding herself of the internalized bias would take time.

The comments from her colleagues were in bad taste, even ignorant, and it takes a toll on someone like Tori, who has constantly had to educate and correct other people when they nonchalantly throw these remarks her way. It makes it harder for Tori to feel at ease and confident or to just shrug it off. How could she not take it personally when she's been holding feelings of resentment or even shame about her own internalized bias?

But it's important to remember in those moments of frustration that people's cognitive dissonance (aka ignorance) is not your problem; it's theirs. It's not about us; it's about *them* and the work *they* need to do. It becomes your problem when you create a narrative about yourself through these experiences. Instead of putting her colleagues' comments in the mental microaggressions box, reporting them to HR or higher-ups, or simply being more direct about her own discomfort, Tori took it on her shoulders. We are wasting precious energy when we get sucked into endlessly questioning why people react the way they do. That energy could go into building the type of middle-aged-white-man confidence and entitlement that we all deserve. We need to efficiently and effectively talk up our value and take up space, instead of getting caught in the energy-sucking minutiae of other people's bias.

Reality check: People out there are ignorant, even good people can be biased, and some people are outright racist (I'm talking to you, email troll lady), so even when they make us *feel* like the other, are we going to let ourselves believe it? For me, Tori's story serves as an example of what many who have felt othered grapple with: letting other people's narratives take over our confidence, whether we realize it consciously or not.

Tori should be able to eat lunch with Asian people, white people, whomever she pleases, while holding the confidence that she's uniquely Tori: Asian American and a talented media manager.

We need to ask ourselves why we repress our duality and for whom. Next time you're met with an off-color comment, a sexist or racist remark, or a statement that makes you uncomfortable, turn the tables. Instead of driving yourself crazy in the moment trying to figure out whether or not you're being too sensitive or holding all that unease inside, shift the power dynamic and get rid of that heavy energy by asking the speaker a question like: *What exactly do you mean by that? Could you explain what you mean? Could you elaborate on what you meant?* Or (my personal favorite), repeat what they say back to them. So in Tori's case, it might sound something like this: *You'd like me to help your daughter with her Chinese homework? Is that because you think I grew up there?*

Questions are powerful because you're essentially giving the other person a chance to register for themselves how inappropriate their comment or action was. Instead of taking up that uncomfortable energy on your own, you're throwing them off-kilter by letting them hear how they sounded, in a direct way, while still keeping your professionalism and your cool. You make your stance clear and leave *them* with the uncomfortable feeling, not you. In addition, this gives you a way to get more information and gather a response. They may apologize or self-correct, and if they're totally oblivious, at least you know where they stand and you can escalate the issue with HR if it's having an impact on your ability to do your work.

In order to shift to a place of power, we also need to be mindful of working on our inner voice and being cognizant of what we allow ourselves to believe about ourselves. How we talk about ourselves to ourselves matters.

Psychologist and researcher Ethan Kross, who studies the science of introspection, has a name for this conundrum: chatter. It's when you replay that comment from a coworker slighting your appearance or intelligence, or when you berate yourself for sending a poorly written email. *Why did I say that? What did they mean with that passing comment? I'm so stupid. I shouldn't have sent that.*

In Tori's case, it was the self-limiting statements she developed as a result of constantly questioning her belonging: *Why are they asking me to help them with these things? Because I'm Asian? I'm different from them. I'll never be seen in the same way.* The way we decide to make assumptions about ourselves, our worth, and what we bring to the table can easily be influenced by comments and digs we ingest from others. It's helpful to take a step back and reframe what the comments mean to us and how we process them. And not necessarily for others, but for ourselves.

For example, instead of giving in to the chatter, Tori could decide to change what she allows herself to believe about herself from that experience: *My boss has got some learning to do about my community. My knowing more than one language gives me an advantage. Yes, I am proudly Asian, but I'm also great at what I do, and I can have many different facets and identities beyond my background.*

Sometimes even the mere idea that there's a potential for bias causes our internal threat alarm to activate our inner chatter. It can feel impossible to walk into a situation as a blank slate—we tend to bring our past experiences along for the ride, particularly those of stigma toward our group. For me, being the only Latina or only immigrant in a room can be instantly triggering. Despite being confident and hardworking, I used to feel constantly tripped up by my own thoughts of self-doubt when I was "the only" in a room. I would sometimes lose track of how I really wanted to show up at my job, not because I was ashamed of my identity but because my defenses went up. I dreaded the feeling of having to explain myself and the pressure to make myself relatable to others, like the onus was on me.

As I've mentioned, I still struggle with the English language, despite having lost my Spanish accent. At work, I've often caught myself mispronouncing common sayings or mixing up my words. Because I've lost my accent—and especially because I work alongside some of the brightest minds in the world—these mispronunciations often make me self-conscious about my intelligence and trigger my inner chatter almost immediately. *I'm not as smart as they are.*

When I first started as a production coordinator at MSNBC, the colleagues I worked with and the guests I helped book were

highly educated, most from Ivy League colleges, and used sophis-
ticated words in email exchanges, such as "vacillate," "behoove,"
and "Pollyanna." Merriam-Webster became my best friend. Ironically, I also feel this way when speaking Spanish. I'll come down
on myself for losing my family's Chilean accent, or bash myself
when I'm unable to express myself to my family as clearly or as
quickly as I'd like.

I never felt like I could *just be*. As much as I've been my own
inner cheerleader, I've also been my worst critic. I'd take being
self-aware too far, and before I knew it, those thoughts about
how to put my best foot forward, how to blend in, what I needed
to do to prove myself, and so on would easily turn into self-
criticism. Yet I was doing the same work as my coworkers. I had
ascended to my position for a reason, and I was equally qualified.
And I was self-aware enough to know where I could grow and
do better work, but I only started to really do that when I locked
in on the source of my insecurity and realized that it was more
about the accumulation of other life experiences I'd had than
about my overall intelligence or adeptness at the job.

It's easy to get caught up in self-judgment or judgments of
others. (I don't want to diminish the numerous times we are on
the receiving end of prejudice due to our race, gender, religion,
sexual orientation, and so on, but we also must be aware of how
those very ideas have been ingrained in our minds and activated,
even when we're not on the receiving end of discrimination.)
Somehow our brains love to latch on to these thoughts more
often than the positive ones. It's hard to part with them. On a
subconscious level, this voice has become part of your identity.

I am a gay Latina who should hide. I am a Black Muslim woman who should play down my beliefs. We've given ground to that self-talk that plays like a broken record. You want to shed it, but getting rid of that voice feels scary. That voice has always been there for you. In some ways, it's been your best ally, your defense team when you were faced with bias and prejudice and your own insecurities. It's familiar. You have such an intimate relationship with that voice that it will likely never fully go away.

So, as those negative, chatty voices try to drag you down, remind yourself of all your goodness, strengths, and accomplishments. Pretend that you're your best friend or cheerleader talking about yourself, and then address the chatter and say to it, "I'll be damned if I'll be made to feel less than." And act while you're in *that* mindset.

Create your own go-to phrase to squash any chatter that could plant seeds of doubt.

"Not my truth."

"That's not me."

"Hell no."

Use your own self-talk language to snap out of any moment that brings a false sense of limited potential your way. The time will come when you realize that you've outgrown that negativity and doubt. You require distance from it in order to evolve. The reality is that your limited self doesn't exist. It's a distillation of the perceptions you assume other people may have of you. That limited self doesn't actually embody who you are. It's not you. It's just a bunch of fleeting thoughts that need to be handled.

We can choose another narrative about ourselves. Even if you feel like your ideas about who you are have been riddled by the stereotypes around you, the only thing that matters is whether you choose to believe them or not. When you remove that layer of inferiority from the equation, you start showing up as a stronger, more effective, clearer asset with the type of confidence that shows others, *I deserve to be here. I don't buy into the perception of the other. My duality is what makes me more valuable.*

In order to use your duality superpower to its full potential, when you feel othered or put in a box as a minority at work, first take the time to identify the uncomfortable moments that make you feel less than and vulnerable, and write them down. For Tori, it was when she was verbally confronted with her Asian roots and the microaggressions that were thrown in the mix. For me, it was knowing I was referred to as "illegal," which seeped into my sense of worth way before the workplace. When we identify what is triggering our feelings, it becomes easier to know where we are directing our energy. It gives us more control. Name it to tame it. You have the power to dictate the narrative about who you are and what you have to offer.

When I faced my own triggers, I'd coach myself through them in the third person: *Okay, Daniela, what are we going to do?* This helped me take a step back and get a better grasp of how to help myself through situations that had felt hopeless. Research shows that referring to yourself in the third person can actually help you distance yourself from the problem that has you tied up in knots and make a difference in emotional self-regulation. This technique will help you end the perpetual emotional chatter and focus on problem-solving more effectively. Somehow it helps remove your emotions from the situation. Whatever you may be going through at work won't last forever. Don't let it have a stranglehold on how you show up. The goal is to draw a careful distinction between your perceived threat of feeling othered and the situation at face value. Recognize what's hindering your ability to be who you are at work, call it out in real time by using the question technique if necessary, and don't be afraid to bring your unique value to the forefront.

When you take the time to self-examine, to do a deep dive on where you've acquiesced in order to fit in and belong, when you become aware of your inner chatter and the sources of your insecurities, you'll be able to start taking charge of your narrative and using your duality as a superpower. You bring a unique life experience and personal story to work that makes you better at your job. For me, I had a personal understanding of the nuances of the immigration system, which better informed me to amplify and highlight different angles of the story that needed to be considered. I had to flip my script and, instead of looking at my duality from a place of inferiority, channel it into confidence and conviction about my work.

What you've been hiding, avoiding, or living in shame about might now actually serve your career and help you succeed if you let it. Think about all the different gifts the experience of seeing things in duality can offer you: emotional intelligence, cultural diversity, empathy, a different viewpoint, life experience, or any other unique part of your personality. Once you identify your own advantage, play up that asset. Stand up straighter while walking in the office halls, speak a little louder, and remember, your existence and identity are yours alone to define. Your indispensable quality is bringing the fullness of who you are to the table. Don't let yourself believe anyone telling you a different story. At the end of the day, fitting in is overrated. It's time to set the tone on how you want to show up at work. Duality is your superpower in getting to your next step. You have something others don't—use it!

6

You Are Worthy

You got your foot in the door—whether that means landing a new job, more access, or a promotion—and you've worked your ass off. But often, once we've graduated to the next level in our careers but still want more, we have the thought that all of our current success could vanish with one wrong move. It's best to stay in this place and be grateful, right? You've likely struggled to get where you are; you've seen the damaging effects of unemployment or unfulfilling jobs; you've also maybe been raised with the idea that working hard and being humble is the greatest trait of all, and your hard work will eventually get noticed. You've had to be twice as good as everyone else. Therefore, you might feel you should just be grateful for the success you've achieved, because it could disappear in a snap.

Many of us get stuck in this "just be grateful" mindset, and it holds us back when we need to be asking for more or pushing to go even further. Often this mindset comes from the conditioning that has been upheld by our abuelitas, mamas, parents, and a whole trail of generational figures.

The grateful mindset started out as a simple reflection of the character and values we were brought up with. Bragging was a no-no, a sign of tackiness. Malos modales—bad form. And of course, if done in the wrong tone, talking about your accomplishments can be a turnoff for a lot of people. But gratitude, luck—these are socially and culturally acceptable ways of viewing your success. Instead of taking pride in the hard work that got us here and learning how to embrace our worth and express our value, we become perpetually grateful to everyone but ourselves. And all the time and energy we've put into our careers can feel overshadowed by our "good luck."

Even to this day, although I know my family is aware of how hard I work, they have a strong sense that fate and luck have had a big part in each of the promotions or achievements in my career. And they believe we owe this streak of good luck all our gratitude. It's how the story of fleeting success is upheld. It's as if we hold on to that eternally grateful mindset because we need to fuel the good vibrations of good luck. As if we need to make good with fate. But there was a level of grittiness, strategy, work, and research that you've had to put in to develop your career. It was deliberate on your part, not just luck.

No one but you will ever really know the amount of stress you go through on your quest to develop your own career. Personally, I've made sacrifices to my personal life, often going without sleep and exercise while writing a book, having a full-time job, and working on several other side hustles. No one else will ever truly know how much effort it took you to get where you are. I say this not to complain but to acknowledge that we have to protect and be very aware of the value we've built through those sacrifices, for that very reason. No one will ever understand your value more than you.

So why are we still relying on luck and fate? Why are we willing to settle for less rather than going after more?

Even though I am conscious of all my sacrifice and efforts, there are parts of me that still carry my family's voice in my head. I have worked my ass off to earn my success, but there still exists that place in my consciousness where I chalk it up to fate. Yet sometimes I hear that voice of caution urging me to not lose this "luck of the draw," nudging me to tread lightly for fear of ruffling feathers and being seen as ungrateful. I've gotten better about this over time, but there has always been a feeling of impermanence about my accomplishments, a sense that if I took even the slightest wrong step, they would slip away.

When you grow up constantly trying to catch up to everyone around you, without access to opportunities, it's easy to feel like you need to show at every moment how grateful you are for everything and everyone. In my case, getting my foot in the door at a major media conglomerate just a few months after receiving DACA laid the perfect groundwork for that mindset, because it was the opportunity of a lifetime.

It was a hot June day with just enough of a breeze to send the dozens of flags around 30 Rockefeller Plaza flapping majestically in the sky. Tourists moved in clusters, stopping mid-walk to whip out their cameras, hoping to capture the area where the iconic skating rink lay, which was now converted into al fresco dining for the warmer months. Slow jazz floated up from the restaurant's enclosed open space below, where executives and higher-ups held meetings over lavish dishes of lobster, sea bass, and white wine.

Above the 30 Rock lobby, José Maria Sert's *American Progress* mural wrapped around the ceiling. Employees buzzed hastily up the escalators from the subway that rumbled underground as I excitedly made my way to the visitor registration center to receive my work badge from a cheerful security employee with a sunny smile. *Pierre*, his nametag read. His thick accent reminded me of my Haitian grandfather's, making me feel right at home. He'd later become my go-to number on speed dial in the mornings during my role at *Morning Joe*, helping me out in a pinch anytime we had VIPs or late-arriving show guests we needed to rush up to the studio to make air.

My first day as an NBC page and those that followed were a full-on crash course on the history of 30 Rock and its shows. I was matched up with other newly selected pages in a start group guided by a current page who had been designated to show us the ropes and train us to do tours, for which we were each handed a hefty folder filled with facts and data we had to learn by heart. As pages, we were ambassadors to the public, visitors, and temporary guests, so we had to exercise professional know-how and be aware of all the protocol and nuances that came with the job, including memorizing the names of all the VIPs and major executives throughout NBCUniversal. We were a trusted resource for just about anything that happened there.

My daily uniform, interactions with everyone from tourists to talent walking the halls, what to do during chance meetings with executives—it was all laid out in exacting detail. And when in doubt, there were a number of resource guides and fellow pages to consult.

My acceptance to the program came only a few weeks before I graduated from college. I was in total shock and disbelief when I answered the call from a 212 area code and heard the program director offering me the job. After hanging up, I ran through the house I shared with my freshman college roommate and her sorority sisters, looking for someone to blurt out the news to. I stormed into the bathroom and startled my roommate, who was still in a bra and head towel, with shrieks of happiness and a full embrace. "Sorry, I should have knocked! But you won't believe what happened!" I couldn't even put words together.

Everything was falling into place, and it was all happening so quickly. About a month after receiving the NBC Page Program call, it was graduation day. As the oldest of my four brothers and sisters and the first of my family to graduate from an American university, I didn't take that moment lightly. The magnitude of it all hit me seconds before I was called up to walk and receive my diploma. Knowing how hard payments would be, I had tried my best to graduate early. I had knocked off a whole year of schooling with college credits transferred over from high school.

That walk to the stage was a symbolic nod to the literal sweat and tears every single member of my family, both those in the United States and those back home in Chile, went through in order to get me to this moment. From the nights my family—parents *and* siblings—worked together to pick up graveyard shifts cleaning movie theaters, to the small amounts of money my grandmothers were able to save up and send my way to keep the hope of graduating alive, to the personal sacrifices I made to get myself there. We were all in this together, and this win was for all of us.

And to say I felt grateful to get my foot in the door at a

world-recognized media brand like NBCUniversal is an understatement. There was so much sacrifice that ultimately culminated in this moment. I saw this job as a saving grace. It felt like they were taking a chance on hiring me and I needed to perpetually show I had earned my spot. I carried that feeling of gratefulness like a badge of honor.

With the serendipitous timing and things somehow falling into place at the eleventh hour, this was, by all means, a product of fate and good luck as far as I was concerned. And my mom and my grandma Mary made sure to remind me of it every chance they got. (I am, after all, a strong believer in my faith.) But this way of thinking laid the groundwork for how I'd see all my future career successes. The story I told myself about how success is fleeting kept roaming in my subconscious—where, as we know, our beliefs are harder to detect and control. I didn't really think about it on the surface. I was just excited to be there and work hard, and I kept hoping fate, luck, or whatever magical force it might be would keep working for me.

Knowing DACA provided just a temporary work permit and the NBC Page Program would only last up to a year, I found myself fighting the feeling that the rug could be pulled out from under me at any moment. My way of controlling my environment was going above and beyond, overcompensating to show how grateful I was. I rotated through different departments and shows as an NBC page, from *Late Night* to the business side of the company, until I ultimately landed a temporary assignment as the page for *Morning Joe*, which, in a matter of months, led to a full-time role there as a production coordinator.

It became very clear that this role on *Morning Joe* would be totally different from what I'd experienced as a page. Sure, I had worked with *Saturday Night Live*, the king of live shows, but I was at the bottom of the hierarchy there, and my experience was limited to what I *observed*, not what I did. But now, a year into the job as a page, I was managing and coordinating the movements of the live show like it was a choreographed dance.

I still remember my first day on the job as production coordinator. The previous show coordinator showed me around backstage and eventually brought me into the dressing room of one of the show's cohosts, Mika Brzezinski, for a quick introduction. I was excited, nervous, and thrilled to own whatever tasks came my way. During my morning tours as a page, I'd seen Mika walking the halls in between commercial breaks as I ushered tourists through the iconic halls of our news studios, handing out historical facts and describing how TV magic is made. I'd see their faces light up as their eyes traced the pictures of famous anchors, which were perfectly lined up in chronological order under the myriad of cables and lights that decorated the news hallway. When Mika walked by, with her tall Louboutin heels and signature platinum pixie cut perfectly in place, I'd giddily whisper to the tour, "That's Mika Brzezinski!"

Oohs and aahs would follow, and she'd graciously exclaim, "Hi! How are you all doing today?," acknowledging our presence as if she knew us. It was her way of making people feel important and seen—one of her many strong suits as a popular news anchor and journalist.

On my first day backstage, I watched as everyone scurried around in a frenzy, putting together final details minutes before the show went live. Guests were shuttled from their greenrooms to hair and makeup, and then rushed on set. Interns scrambled down long hallways hailing last-minute wardrobe requests. PAs rushed hot-off-the-printer scripts to the hosts in preparation for the show. The sense of urgency and precision of it all was right up my alley.

Oddly enough, it felt familiar—always running places, feeling a sense of urgency. For better or worse, that's how I grew up. I found myself having mini flashbacks to the times I was late for practice or a game as a result of our old car breaking down (it was the cheapest option on the used lot); running across Times Square to make it in time for my Bad Boy interview after an eighteen-hour bus ride with nine stops along the way, which came in behind schedule; running back to the office during my internship after walking dogs during my lunch break. I could go on. I was in a never-ending loop of perpetually rushing and running, holding on to what was in front of me as if it were already almost gone.

The idea of sitting still or doing just one job or doing no more than what was asked of me felt like a danger zone. Overcompensating felt safe because it minimized the possibilities of having only one source of income to depend on; if I had three jobs, it meant I'd stay afloat even if my hours were cut at one of them or my earnings were less than usual one week. Having experienced how close I could come to losing opportunities to advance in my education and then my career, taking on at least three jobs at once was what felt appropriate.

That mentality followed me in my professional life as I climbed the ladder at my corporate job. That meant that when I landed one solid full-time job, I was always looking for ways to do more than my job description asked of me, so that I'd have data points to use in negotiations for the next step. Perhaps it was exactly because of that that I was always running toward something (literally and figuratively), fighting for my chance, scrappily getting it done. Back then, so much was on the line. Yet, in my professional life, this hasty rhythm my body knew so well translated into a sense of urgency that my bosses were quick to appreciate.

I was grateful to have the opportunity to get the coffees, print the scripts, fetch last-minute clothing items for set, and master the minutiae of talent requests. My goal was to outwork everyone else around me, searching for any opportunity to set myself apart from the rest of the revolving door of production assistants, interns, and coordinators. That was front and center in my mind when, after the rest of my backstage tour, the show's coordinator eventually brought me into Mika's dressing room for a quick introduction.

Amid the commotion of getting ready in the dressing room, Mika welcomed me to the team and then quickly followed up by asking me if I was the one who would be getting her coffee in the mornings.

"Yes!" I proudly exclaimed.

She kiddingly responded, "Good...you better not fuck it up!"

Laughter filled the room. I nodded back with a nervous smile. Her statement, although said in jest, kind of shook me. It was also an aha moment: I recognized that getting her coffee right would be an opportunity to gain her trust and to stand out. For someone like Mika—who works around the clock, often late into the night, and has wake-up calls at three in the morning every day to cohost a three- or sometimes four-hour live show without breaks—coffee is key to getting through the long and busy day. And I was all over it.

Every weekday, I set my alarm fifteen minutes early to get my tasks for studio prep out of the way before quickly rushing down to the ground floor of 30 Rock and taking my post next to the Starbucks door, which I would start banging on ten minutes before it opened. I'd plead with the barista to open early and was usually met with rolled eyes: *Oh God, there she is again.* I knew that this little song and dance allowed me to have Mika's coffee—a "black eye" misto, extra hot, extra foam—in hand just in time for her I'm here text, which meant she was approaching the side lobby doors to be escorted up to the studios. "Good morning, Mika," I'd say, keeping it brief to avoid talking her ear off. Then I'd place the coffee cup in her hands while walking by her side toward the turnstiles, edging ahead to the elevator to eliminate any waiting time, and swiftly escort her up to her dressing room in one fell swoop.

When I say I focused on getting her the best coffee possible, I mean I did it like my life depended on it, as silly as that sounds, because I knew it was a lifeline to her day. "That coffee will either make or break me," she'd say. When I say I constructed a process around this all-important coffee order, I mean it! It was a whole thing.

Although it may sound ridiculous because it's just coffee, at that stage in my career, it was my little trick to move forward strategically, a creative competitive advantage that helped me stand out and get noticed. Mika took note of the level of attention and intensity I put into this detail that others might have completely overlooked. The next thing I knew, Mika started taking me under her wing, asking me to fill in for assistants or accompany her to different industry events and functions where I got to really expand my professional Rolodex; from fashion shows to offsite shoots, I was being introduced to high-profile individuals and influencers along the way. Soon, my responsibilities at the show quickly became larger and more complex.

It's all about finding our aha moment—the one that provides a path for us to differentiate ourselves from the pack, an opportunity we make our own that will help plant the seed to give us an edge and make us indispensable.

What was meant to be a three-month assignment at *Morning Joe* transitioned into a full-time position in less than a month and a half. The show was very short-staffed at the time, so when I accepted the production coordinator job, it actually turned out to be three roles in one. I went from handling basic tasks to dealing with guest logistics, hearing the executive producer and other senior staff yelling in my ear from the control room for answers to questions that the live show depended on. I was the eyes, ears, and coordinator of all movements on set and backstage with guests. I also had to learn how to delegate in real time while keeping the puzzle pieces together to help execute other production details vital to the show. Making one wrong move or being one second too late threw everything off.

Needless to say, at first, my experience didn't really match up to the requirements, so I had to figure it out *fast*. And I did. This job made use of the soft skills I had learned in my endless side hustles, plus my newfound know-how in the media industry, working with high-profile personalities, and being accommodating with a sense of urgency. I was riding high on the achievement of landing this job, getting my foot in the door, and being validated for doing well at it.

Then I got promoted to a junior booking position. It was a role that had been created from scratch with little precedent in terms of expectations. That meant I now worked on a relatively small team where everyone was focused on getting their work done in this fast-moving, deadline-driven environment—as a result, there was little time for guidance. I had to learn on the go. I had to earn my place all over again in a totally new way. Following orders was no longer the only key to success. If I wanted to do well in this new role, I would have to learn how to take initiative and help craft the position. I needed to think beyond getting the small stuff perfect, getting the coffee *just right*. I went from running around in a studio all day to being in front of a computer for nine to ten hours a day.

Suddenly, my steady confidence was faltering under the pressure of my insecurities. I wasn't just the only woman on the editorial planning team; I was also the only immigrant, and the youngest one there. I felt constantly behind the curve. And slowly, doubt began to creep into my thoughts and make me question if I should even be there. But I forged ahead, focusing on all the ways I had strategized to get ready for this moment.

I had looked up to several career role models throughout the years, hoping to replicate their confidence and demeanor once I got to a more senior role. I wanted to emulate the assertive way the executives back at Bad Boy Entertainment discussed ideas, or the ease in delegating and natural poise shown by my

Australian boss at the same company. I practiced getting rid of "likes" and "ums" in my everyday speech so I'd sound more professional. I started speaking in a lower voice register to seem more mature.

Then, when it actually came time to put it all into practice in the real world of corporate America, when the stakes were high and I was beginning to deal directly with my bosses, I choked. In my quest to nail the right tone, I was putting on a mask, a performance of how I wished I could show up, and I was good at it. But as the months rolled on, I began to feel uncomfortable in my own skin. I was in a perpetual loop of excessive gratefulness and reactivity to my superiors.

I figured if I just tiptoed around what I thought was expected of me, I could still find success in remaining under the radar and simply getting the work done. And that's exactly what I did for the first few years in this role—I reverted back to what I knew: *Put your head down. Do the work. Make yourself useful, needed, and valued. Stick to what you know, Daniela.* But then, instead of offering up my ideas in editorial meetings, I'd overcompensate by saying something like, "Does anyone need any coffee?" (Mind you, this was no longer part of my job.) It's one thing to do this once in a blue moon, but really I was hiding behind menial work for some sort of safety. But it's doing this sort of "office work," when we are beyond those administrative roles or lower positions, that will continue to negatively exacerbate the power dynamics at work. I was selling myself short. And it was affecting my psyche; the tiptoeing, self-censorship, and just-grateful-to-be-here mentality started causing me to miss out on editorial meetings I should have asked to join. I also didn't ask to be a part of them for fear of being impolite or crossing a line that would ruffle feathers. I didn't want to put my position at risk. Without being fully aware, I was reinforcing a power dynamic that kept me from appearing less senior by downplaying my skills.

Rather than asserting myself in my new booking role, I hoped that eventually someone would take me by the hand, recognize all my hard work, and tell me when and what I needed to do to get to the next step. But we know that's almost never the case, nor should we sit around waiting for that. The more high-stakes our roles become, the less hand-holding we'll get from our superiors and the more we've got to work to take the reins and set the tone in our careers. Everyone around you has their own things to worry about and their own jobs to do. We can and should ask for help and support, but we shouldn't wait for someone to jumpstart our career development.

At times I wondered if I had enough knowledge to do the job. I mean, was I really qualified to pre-interview a former president or the secretary general of NATO? Of course I was! I had been hired for a reason, and deep down I knew I had the chops. But the baggage of a poor undocumented immigrant's narrative continued to interfere nonsensically in my head: *I'm not as smart as these people.* I felt this way despite having earned a degree in international studies with a foreign policy concentration. My qualifications and what was going on in my head didn't match each other, but I didn't quite know how to get them on the same page.

I can't tell you how many times I've spoken to women in my mentorship community who have the same type of thoughts about their qualifications. Most have advanced degrees and/or experience to spare, yet they still feel like they lack the knowledge to show up with more authority and power to their jobs.

One particular mentee comes to mind: Estefania. She was young and eager to learn from the other women in her group, and when the time came to practice introducing themselves and their careers, she kept it brief: "I work at a company that specializes in 3D medicine." It took a full hour for her to mention to the group that she was actually the founder and CEO of the company she said she "worked at," a 3D prosthetics company in South America. We were all stunned. This was merely an introduction to a group of women she'd be engaging with in a space that was intended to help her grow professionally for the following months, so the stakes weren't high, but can you imagine the missed opportunity this would have been elsewhere?

It could have meant missing out on an investing opportunity or a potential partnership that might help her company. You never know who you're going to meet or when the moment will call for people to turn to you and give you the floor. "I didn't want it to come off as bragging or off-putting," she told me. She felt out of her league as a woman founder, like she didn't fit the description of what someone in her position was supposed to look like, sound like, or act like. Owning those words—CEO and founder—felt icky. They felt like big shoes she told herself she couldn't fit into yet. The story she had created—*I won't be taken seriously*—was upheld by her own limiting beliefs about herself: she looked young, she was a woman in an industry heavily dominated by men in South America, she needed more years in the industry, and so on. Mind you, in her country, machismo is rampant in business, and the sexism and bias around women in the workplace is even more severe than it is in the United States, all of which had made her even more used to downplaying her skills and role.

Yet there she was, succeeding in that role! She was hustling on designing the product, raising capital, and overseeing operations, and, of course, she was the face of the company.

I understand Estefania. I also felt out of my league. In the most inopportune moments, when I should've been offering insight or actively participating, I'd suddenly become overwhelmed with the sense that it would just be a matter of time until my chance was over; they'd figure out I really didn't have the skills needed for my role and replace me with someone who did. I latched on to the "be polite" and "know my place" mentality instead; I used old rules to find safety.

Without even realizing it, I was experiencing what is widely known as "impostor syndrome," a term that was coined in 1978 by psychologists Pauline Rose Clance and Suzanne Imes. It's used to express the feeling that while everyone around you got where they are by merit, you're an impostor whose success is a mistake or the fruit of luck. That *Holy hell, how did I get here, and when will I get caught and be told I don't belong here?* feeling. In their research, Clance and Imes cite "certain early family dynamics and later introjection of societal sex-role stereotyping" as a significant contributor to the development of this feeling of being a phony. It turns out that our sense of identity in the context of our upbringing is a good indicator of the origin of this syndrome.

Let's say you grew up constantly being compared to a sibling or cousin who was more adept than you at school or other activities, being told that you wouldn't be able to measure up to them, and it impacted how you saw yourself and your competencies.

Even though you may not believe your family's assertions to be true, there might be an unconscious part of you that is still working to prove them wrong so as to refute this misconception about who you are and what you are capable of doing.

A second form of social expectation that exacerbates impostor syndrome, according to Clance and Imes, is being told you're all that and then some while growing up. That you can do anything you want in the world and that the world will love you back no matter what. This overload of praise might be a point of hesitancy for you, leading you to doubt the source of admiration when you actually start experiencing difficulty achieving goals. You were told that everything you did was perfect, so when you do experience hiccups along the way, the feeling of failure is magnified. Deviating from perfection can be scary for you because it feels like it's what's expected of you.

I likely fall somewhere between both of these. I spent a great amount of energy trying to disprove the world's ideas about the limits of my success due to how I grew up socioeconomically and my status as the other. On the other hand, my immigrant family always set me up to think I had a natural ease for succeeding, from learning English quickly to performing well academically to getting myself involved in school activities (all things I had to work really hard on). And although they didn't incessantly floor me with a million compliments, there was a clear expectation that I, as the oldest and most type A child in the family, would be the one to attain the American Dream. The psychological weight of our career choices is not just ours, but that of our whole family. I carry that burden proudly, but it doesn't mean I don't feel the emotional cost that comes with it.

While it's estimated that 70 percent of women and men will suffer from impostor syndrome at some point in their life, there is evidence that shows minority communities are disproportionally affected. However, I hesitate to put the full blame for our difficulties on this concept alone, knowing the very real barriers and lack of access that percolate from the top down and stand in the way of our advancement, especially that of many women—namely, systemic variables like classism, prejudice, biases, sexism, and racism. Let's also be really clear about the fact that it falls heavily on leadership within workplaces to create a sense of belonging and inclusion for women of color to feel like they have real equity when they walk in at work. And as important as that is for your growth, it's not always the case. It's important to pause and also question the idea of imposter syndrome being of our own doing, and make room for explanations as to *why* you might feel this way. Let's not discard the feelings of doubt that come through being on the receiving end of microaggressions, gaslighting, and working at a company that portrays a false sense of inclusivity efforts.

As a result of all this, we may react to our environment by constantly trying to seek validation for our efforts and allowing our sense of value to be defined by others. We may start thinking, *If I play into what others think or expect of me, it'll be easier for me to succeed and prove that I'm capable.*

Sounds oddly familiar for us shape-shifters, doesn't it?

We may find ourselves working overtime when we don't need to, just to show how hard we can work. Taking on administrative tasks because we can get them done efficiently and it takes the burden off of others, even if such tasks are no longer part of our job description. Doing these little things right and feeling needed guarantees one thing: gratification. In my case, early on, it helped me feel validated, because up until then, I believed it was what made my higher-ups want to keep me around. I had survived in my environment by staying in my lane. Hell, I was just happy I had a lane to exist in. But now I was at a different point in my career, and wasn't acting like it.

If self-monitoring and overcompensation were my MO, then praise and validation had become the reward for that behavior. I found relief and success in being accepted, because it validated my sense of belonging, the one I'd been on a constant search for.

"Good job, Daniela" was the phrase that sent my dopamine levels through the roof. It was a nod that made me feel like I was on the right track. That I belonged. It didn't matter if my identity felt like a mirage, so long as it reflected those around me. Belonging would open doors, bring opportunities for advancement; it held the promise of breaking the cycle of the barriers of generational inequity I faced. More importantly, belonging became a rite of passage, something even more important and powerful for someone with my background. It was like getting even with history, armoring me with validation. So, even though I might not necessarily need it to corroborate my *personal* worth, validation has been the green light for my professional advancement. It's something that I have to work consistently on combating.

From the early days of being recognized for my achievements at school—like being the first of my school to win the accelerated reader program in the fifth grade—to seeking out opportunities to take on multiple professional projects, to keeping that hardworking immigrant yes-girl alive (everyone seemed to like and be receptive to her), validation had been my way of assimilating. It was part of the gold star reward system that made me feel like I belonged to my environment. It was a source of stability amid the uncertainty caused by my legal and cultural limbo.

I was hooked on the rush of checking things off my list and piling on to-dos, because the promise at the peak of the adrenaline rush was a stamp of approval. In many ways, the praise and validation felt like an acknowledgment of my contributions in a country that, to this day, is always questioning my worthiness as an immigrant. Consciously or not, that was how I approached my work.

I wanted to create a path for myself that my family and ancestors couldn't even dream of. On the surface, it all had to do with creating success and overcoming my environments. Finding and building individual equity, financial independence, career success, and self-sufficiency. Beating the odds. Building a successful life and breaking generational restrictions and constraints of all kinds. Self-actualizing.

I had big lofty goals and the inner trust to go with it. *Nothing can stop me,* I thought. And I aimed to prove myself to the gatekeepers, the naysayers, anyone who thought I was too different from them. If I put all my energy into proving how worthy I was at every step of the way, I'd get to where I needed to be. My need for validation came from wanting to feel protected from being different, not from my lack of confidence. I didn't want to miss out on opportunities or be passed up solely because I didn't fit the mold. I found safety in strategizing and coming up with whatever performative methods I needed to earn someone's good impression of me. To feel worthy of it.

I'd keep a watchful eye on the news cycle and would become all ears whenever DACA would make the headlines (too many times to count), because I wanted to make sure I continued to fit into the box of "model minority." Unfortunately, this can exacerbate stereotypes and be harmful for the rest of our community. *Look at us, we're doing great things! Contributing in really big ways—we're doctors, Pulitzer Prize–winning writers, engineers, lawyers! See, we belong!* These are all great things, of course, and we do contribute in big ways, but it's an enormous strain on our lives when we need to constantly validate ourselves through our success and productivity to make sure other people recognize that we, as immigrants or women of color, belong—even when we know that this very sense of belonging is actually hanging by the political thread of a pathway for legalization.

The livelihoods of DACA recipients are on a constant roller coaster of lawsuits that have the power at any moment to take away our ability to be here legally or equally. But we persevere regardless. And while most of you might not have as specific an example of legal constraints as the ones that made it hard for me to integrate fully in this country, you might have experience knowing what it's like to be on the receiving end of legal prejudice because of your skin color, culture, language, religion, socioeconomic status, sexual orientation, or other factors. We may internalize this as if something really is wrong with us and find ways to be validated to make up for any differences we feel are liabilities. I used praise for my accomplishments as a tool for integration.

Listen, there's nothing bad about wanting to go above and beyond, especially in the first few years of your career. It can manifest itself in wonderful qualities for bright-eyed entry-level staffers—"passionate, eager to learn, hardworking." Putting in the grunt work during your first steps in your career earns respect, it shows you're a team player, and it serves a purpose. But as your career expands, going from a supportive role to a leadership, executive, or management role, you can no longer depend on someone's pat on the back, compliments, or good graces to get ahead. It's going to be a must that you get outside of your comfort zone.

I know because it happened to me. As an editorial producer, I could no longer get my validation from the customer-service skills I had used as a page or production coordinator. Suddenly there was a whole new set of skills that I needed to develop, and I didn't know where to begin. I could no longer rely on the hustle culture of buzzing around and getting everyone's errands, drink orders, and wardrobe requests just right. The hustle mentality equated my value to my productivity.

Being a production coordinator was a perfect fit for this. There was a protocol to follow, and my rule-setting tendencies and hustle thrived on it. Like clockwork, I'd wake up at 3:30 a.m., when the rest of the city was not yet fully awake. I felt empowered in the stillness of the night, flooded with a sense of exhilaration as I sat in the cab that drove me from my apartment through the tunnel in Grand Central, which gave way to the towering buildings of Midtown Manhattan. By the time I arrived at 30 Rock, I already had a lengthy to-do list: filing through newspapers, printing scripts, delegating tasks to the interns, prepping the greenrooms, grabbing coffee orders, and more. Then there were three to four hours of nonstop live television I'd coordinate and manage. I was the eyes and ears of the studio for the executives and producers in the control room. I'd man car logistics while greeting guests and tending to talent requests, on the set and off. I'd move through all of it, once again, like a well-choreographed dance.

I managed to develop a system for everything, and a job well done meant that whole live show went off without a hitch: guests arrived on time, hosts and talent were taken care of and happy, and the control room received a play-by-play on everything happening behind the scenes in order to keep every second of the live show in sync. I knew how to be efficient and helpful. I continued to prove to myself and to others how productive I was. The protocols, cues, and rules on the job quickly became second nature to me. They kept everyone happy, including me. Part of me still felt like they were doing me a favor by just giving me an opportunity to move up the ladder. I was overly grateful, even though I knew I had worked hard to get there. The more productive I was, the more accomplished I felt. But eventually I realized that the nonstop hamster wheel I was on wasn't getting me where I wanted to go.

It took me until recently to really understand this lesson: our value is not equal to our productivity. Productivity without a purpose leaves us feeling breathless, exhausted, and at times even defeated, given the aimlessness of our efforts. We'll dive deeper into defining our purpose in chapter 8. For now, I just want you to get off the hamster wheel and start creating small, attainable career development goals for yourself to break the excessive gratefulness and overcompensation patterns you might have dug yourself into as a means of success.

Here's a practical thing that I do when it feels like I'm in overcompensation mode, toiling through everything for everyone in order to feel validated in my role while not really building my own professional brand effectively. Start by laying out all your work duties, projects, and daily to-do lists. Then, keeping in mind your career development, rank them from most to least important. First, you'll find that some of your tasks are there because they really are part of your job—even if you might not *love* doing them. These should rank high because...well, they're your job. Then you might identify other tasks that you take on purposely to learn an added skill. List those next. Now look at what's left over. What are they doing there? Why are you the go-to person for those tasks or projects? Are they essential to your job? Will they help advance your career? Will they aid you in your performance review? If the answer is no, it's time to reevaluate them.

If you're struggling or feel you're not advancing as quickly as you want at work, maybe you can delete some of this gratuitous labor. Maybe it's time to have a bigger conversation with yourself and then your boss. Sometimes our higher-ups don't always remember what we do or what goes into it. They could use a reminder, especially if you've been in your role for a while and the nature or output of your work has changed. Keep them updated. Check in. Don't assume they will. They may not be aware that you're still the one in charge of these extra projects until you mention it to them. Those are the type of work duties that may keep you stuck in the forever-grateful, overcompensating MO. It's time to figure out how to take them off your plate so you can make room for bigger career-building opportunities.

And just to be clear, I'm not saying now's the time to put your foot down on *all* extra duties. Sometimes getting to the next step is all about taking on work outside of your job description to show others you're ready to take on more and have evidence to prove how you've already started to do so. And, let's be frank, if your team is going through a rough patch, it *is* helpful for you to be the one that rolls up their sleeves and gets the job done when no one else is stepping up. The key is being strategic about what you take on and keeping track of your receipts for negotiation talks, so that you don't just work harder, you work smarter.

When the stock of our value is going up, we need to practice sharing our worth and successes out loud. We have to get used to talking about our achievements without feeling like we're being excessively boastful. You have to let people know that it isn't just luck, it's that you're a true *boss*. Start bringing your accomplishments up to your friends, family, and peers. This will help you begin to recognize your own value and embrace it when you're in other arenas. If you're not sure how to approach this or it feels like a foreign language to talk about yourself in this way, start with something simple: "I'm really proud of myself because I managed to…" or "I'm really happy because I was able to…"

Celebrating your achievements doesn't turn you into a bragging monster! And by the way, when we feel like we're bragging, we're usually not, so do it and do it often. When you take the reins of your own life and make things happen for you and those around you, it's okay to pat yourself on the back for what you've done so far. You better believe I will always be proud of every single side door I've managed to creak open. And so should you. We have to remind ourselves that being grateful and being damn proud of ourselves can coexist.

Those moments of pausing, acknowledging, and taking in your wins—however small—help cement the self-confidence you'll need throughout your career. If you ever feel unworthy or skeptical about your value or contributions, this is especially important for you, because it's a reminder that you've earned your spot at the table. You deserve to be there. What's more, celebrating the small wins isn't just beneficial to your sense of self-confidence and self-worth; it can also boost your work life.

In their book *The Progress Principle*, Teresa Amabile and Steven Kramer write about how minor milestones and ordinary or incremental progress within your work organization can set you up psychologically for larger professional wins. With each success, you physiologically activate the reward system in your brain. The more you can activate that reward system, even in small ways, the more that information of self-worth and confidence, which allowed you to do those things in the first place, gets stored in your brain. That release of dopamine increases your motivation and helps set you up for success time after time.

Next, remind yourself that this validation should come from you. After years of living in duality, my need for validation ("Good job!") and belonging ("You're one of us!") began to feel tethered to my professional and personal identity. Affirmation from others can be a useful data point on how to get work done, and it's a great ego boost to be told you're doing a good job, but it's not necessary to do your job well and advance in your career.

You may feel confident enough and have enough trust in yourself to have laser vision and go after a goal. But at the same time, if you're like me, the approval of others—whether I like to admit it to myself or not—can get confused with an essential part of my inner motivation. I started to become more aware of how I reacted to validation. I realized that if I expected validation and didn't receive it, it began to affect my mood. I'd find myself in a slump. I'd lose my energy, thinking about all the possible ways the feedback wasn't what I was expecting and how I could perfect my work in order to receive the affirmation I needed to move forward. But when you're the only or the first, you may never receive the type of validation you're looking for externally. The reality is, you'll come across management, colleagues, or clients who have preconceived notions about your leadership ability or the quality of your work value simply because of your race, gender, sexual orientation, background, and so on.

Ruchika Tulshyan, an author and diversity and inclusion expert who wrote the now-viral piece in *Harvard Business Review*, "Stop Telling Women They Have Imposter Syndrome," told me, "Feeling self-doubt absolutely exacerbates when you're among the only [at work] and research is clear that feelings of imposter syndrome are far more pronounced in people of color than white people. Knowing this can help you stop seeking external validation and finding our own self-worth in a system that wasn't designed for us in mind."

Coming face-to-face with the reality of this dynamic means addressing the internalized cost of seeing our worth through the eyes of others. It means admitting to ourselves that, despite our best efforts to deny it, we've been seeking validation from those who were on the receiving end of our contributions. Somewhere along our journeys, even though the perfectionist tendencies that some of us hold may have fooled us into believing we were in control, we've actually given away the power we hold over our own sense of worth, and we now need to let go of ways of operating that no longer serve us.

This is how we go from reactive in our jobs to proactive.

If we're stuck seeking constant validation, there's no room for growth. And worse yet, it discourages us from really being able to contribute meaningfully, because we've stopped ourselves from using and fine-tuning our voice. That voice is the same voice that's going to keep us moving ahead—our success is incumbent upon it. We need to transform validation and approval into data points that offer positive feedback without allowing them to rule our worth and success. You don't need someone else to tell you that you're doing a good job in order to acknowledge it for yourself.

Shift the power dynamics at work. Act like you deserve to be there. In Spanish we say, "Date tu lugar" or "Hazte respetar." They're phrases we first commonly hear when talking about romantic relationships, advice doled out by our girlfriends and mothers along the lines of "Stand your ground" and "Command respect." These expressions urge us to show our potential partner that we're worthy, valuable, and deserving of respect. We need to do the same thing at the companies we work for, with our higher-ups and even our colleagues. Acting like we belong here doesn't mean overcompensating at every turn to show others our worth. It means shifting our demeanor to embracing our value so that we can take up space with more gravitas.

The time has come for you to stop and acknowledge that *you* are the one who got you this far. Be grateful for the luck or fate that might have helped you along the way, if that's something you believe in, but let's not *lead* with it. Let's be conscious of how much of our success and worth we're giving up to that ideology.

Once you shed that sense of feeling like you owe everyone for your success, like you're an impostor in the space you've earned, you'll learn to validate your own worth instead of needing to find it externally. Then you'll be able not just to dream big but also to plant the seeds of the actions that will effectively help you get there. Fostering your self-confidence and your sense of self-worth along your career and life path will arm you with the strength to show others that you're worth it, you're proud of what've you done, and you mean business.

7

The Burnout

I had been hardwired to play for the short game. Always in survival mode. Pile on the work—the more, the better! Survival mode affects everything, not just the way you show up at work. It can impact things like your health, your mood, and your level of concentration. It can set off a stream of stress hormones. Everything feels reactive. The deadline is now. It's all urgent. Overwhelming. Under this duress, our amygdala—the area of the brain that helps our emotional processing—sends a signal of distress to the command center of the brain, the hypothalamus. When the fight-or-flight response is activated, it releases cortisol. Chronically high levels of cortisol, which occur the more we experience this response to stress, are linked to high blood pressure, anxiety, depression, heart disease, and gut issues. What this means is that chronic survival mode can affect both our physical and our emotional states without us even realizing it. Research shows that the long-term effects of living in a state of emergency can damage your health in a substantial way.

When chaos, crisis, or trauma is at play, and it happens on an ongoing basis, it triggers the body's fight-or-flight response—a mechanism intended to help us get through stressful situations. I had lived with it for so long that my body started to become used to it. Then all of a sudden, it hits you: The weight of working tirelessly at the same company, in the same role, becomes unbearable. Your energy is seeping from your body. Exhaustion takes the place of your enthusiasm. You continue to pull yourself forward. In a strange way, survival mode becomes your support system, your safe space. But when you look up from your desk, you realize your colleagues have managed to move ahead, up the ladder, and you've been too nearsighted. Survival mode can mean being highly efficient at your job, but eventually that constant flow of adrenaline, the rush to take care of the here and now, clouds your vision of the future and doesn't allow you the space to imagine and strategize for the long game. Over time, that constant stress response can also impair our ability to problem-solve, because our mental resources are focused on abstract planning and catastrophizing.

Even on a physiological level, my body had become an expert at fighting stressors. I couldn't go a day without it. I'd see a task, a problem to solve, an opportunity to volunteer, and my body responded with adrenaline and energy, ready to fight small fires. When I got my job at MSNBC, we were doing a traveling show in Chicago, when Mika found out minutes before running to a public event that she'd forgotten her entire makeup bag in New York. Before she could finish her sentence, I was frantically rushing up and down Michigan Avenue, choosing colors and swatches for every makeup need, calling her assistants and makeup artists to get the exact matches, and getting back just in the nick of time before she had to leave. I thrived on high-pressure situations, even if they were trivial. I look back now and wonder: Had I become so used to that rush that I actively looked for these opportunities to come to the rescue? There is always a time and place to roll up your sleeves and get the job done without excuses if the moment calls for it, and this was one of those times, but staying in that constant workhorse mode tends to hold us back rather than help us grow professionally.

Many of us have missed a window of time to advocate for our next step on the career ladder because we were too busy organizing the office closet or raising our hands to finish the administrative work, telling ourselves it would make everyone's life easier, not realizing that it was indeed making everyone's life easier... except our own. These are the catch-22s that lead us to feel stuck in our careers at some point without understanding how we got there. Didn't we go above and beyond to get the job done? Didn't we take on the impossible and refrain from uttering one word of complaint so that our colleagues and bosses could clearly see us as team players?

It's easy to get caught up in the rat race, constantly feeling the need to move forward, searching for success at every turn, fearing the "could've, would've, should've" abyss ripe with scenarios that spike and trigger our stress production.

During my first years employed at NBCUniversal, with DACA in hand, I felt like I had a fresh start on life in some ways. But at the same time, even when my everyday interactions didn't require me to address questions about my status or my upbringing, my body had already conditioned itself both physically and mentally to preempt it. It's like I defaulted to a state of high alert, ready to take a protective stance and dodge questions about my background or strategically maneuver my way around them. My otherness wasn't just a feeling; it had found physical permanence in my body. Every time someone asked me where I grew up, when I moved to the United States, what growing up in Chile or Ohio was like, "How long was that flight?," or any questions in that ballpark, my body immediately reacted: shoulders tensed, stomach churning, jaw clenched, heart racing. There was an acute sense of exhaustion constantly hovering over me, but I chose to ignore it. I didn't question the fight-or-flight response because it had become normalized, in the same way you might get used to a fire alarm that goes off all the time in a kitchen with poor ventilation.

And the worst part was that even though I knew that oftentimes the questioning was polite or part of a casual conversation, that the other person's intention wasn't to pry, my physical reactions still appeared like clockwork. Small talk, first-time interactions, networking—all the regular social interplay that you expect and should jump on at the start of your career—would trigger me. As much as I wanted to be carefree, casual, and easygoing, it was hard for me to lighten up. While trying to display a breezy attitude, I had to fight against the anxiety that was constantly under the surface. And it would eventually catch up with me.

I carried the weight of the critical repercussions on my family's livelihood due to our legal status, and it manifested itself physiologically. A few years ago, I experienced torturous acute vertigo for three days straight, which my doctor attributed to stress and inflammation. I had triggers, sure, but it was also the accumulation of a number of different unchecked whirlwind habits that exploded at the most inopportune times. I was going from one thing to the next, working on survival-mode autopilot, checking things off my list, and piling on the most I could. I was wringing myself dry searching for purpose.

Like many others who are the "firsts" of their families—who have built their sense of self on rising above the barriers in front of them—I was unable to recognize that my work habits were a reaction to the lack of intergenerational opportunities I witnessed in my family. I felt guilty for the sacrifices my family endured and for hearing my own needs too loudly.

I also had not properly learned a mechanism to feel emotions without judgment. If I dared to complain about anything back at home, no matter how big or small, the women in my family always made sure to point out that there were only better days ahead. We were "the lucky ones." That extra-positive outlook is a classic in many Latino families. Surrounded by people who are great at pushing hard and long enough to not feel vencidos, defeated, we're constantly forcing each other to turn our frowns upside down. ¡No te estreses! (Don't stress out!) ¡Podría ser peor! (It could be worse!) Or, my favorite: ¡Sonríe y deja de pensar así! (Just smile and stop thinking so negatively!) As if I loved having those thoughts.

Those messages deepened the sense of guilt and shame I had when I did find myself struggling. And because, generally speaking, Latinos aren't the best example of a group that has reckoned with their own mental health battles, I figured all I could do was exactly what I had been told—in times of sadness or dismay, I suppressed my feelings and tried smiling my way through it all. But that tactic made these unprocessed feelings eventually rear their ugly heads in different ways I couldn't identify or control. It gave me an extremely small window for grieving any shortcomings. There was no time or space to process my feelings. I'd sweep them under the rug and move on. And I didn't know any better. I was stuck in a loop of guilt and shame and bottled-up emotions that eventually erupted like spewing hot lava. My wake-up call didn't come from a specific trigger at work but rather from a buildup of a series of those unattended thoughts. Pushing it all down and then feeling anger and impotence about the repressed emotions was the only emotional reaction my brain would lend itself to.

Mental health is not something that comes easily to any of us. It implies a tug-of-war with our families' values, their upbringings and beliefs versus our new realities. It means having the strength to break with these ties and ask for help.

Mental health is oftentimes something that isn't discussed in minority communities. Among Latinos, it's largely still very much taboo. And we can't place full blame on our parents. Most of our parents, like my mom, were never openly taught about mental health. Feelings were to be suppressed; they got in the way of what needed to be done. That's been the lesson passed on from generation to generation. The focus was on surviving, taking care of your family, paying the bills, keeping up with appearances, not losing the jobs that were hard to come by. We didn't even know how to *begin* talking about our emotions and mental health—the format didn't exist.

Even the way my mom responded to my episodes of frustration was likely a mirroring of how she taught herself (unhealthily) to deal with her own emotional peaks and valleys. It wasn't until she watched me reach my breaking point that she finally understood that seeking help is important and that you can do so before you have a full-on anxiety attack in Midtown. Breaking the generational cycle is not easy, but it can start with you. Identifying our emotions, our issues, and our limiting beliefs will strengthen our relationships with ourselves, which will in turn give way to helping us find our voices and create the mental space to realize we do not need to constantly live in survival mode.

Examining where I had left my own mental health unattended helped me start making corrections on how to better show up for myself and others. I began to ask myself: Where and how have I wrung myself dry? Do I feel overwhelmed or stuck? How has all of this affected my outlook on my goals and career? Has culture or an intergenerational stigma played a role in my ability to manage mental health?

First off, don't be afraid to seek help. Getting access to the right therapist or professional takes time, effort, and work. When you're focused on surviving and working tirelessly around the clock, carving out that extra time to take care of yourself can feel unimaginable. Even now, trying to find that balance can sometimes overwhelm me, but I'm committed to it. I think about how much better it would've been to find healthy ways to cope with what I was going through before reaching the point of combustion, to learn how to not take things so personally. I try to make it my priority to prevent future burnouts.

Something no one told me but that I want you to know is

that finding the right therapist makes a world of difference. Take
your time with it. If the person you see isn't cutting it for you, try
someone else. To be honest, after endless *there's not much they're
going to tell me about myself that I don't already know* self-talk, I
finally mustered up the courage to seek a therapist… and I didn't
connect with the first one I found. Sure, I was disappointed. I
could've easily given up, but I decided my search for another
therapist was a smart investment in myself. So I kept looking and
finally found someone who doesn't just have a method I appreciate but also actually makes me feel calmer, more centered, and
overall better. Discovering data points about yourself, identifying
your triggers, and finding practical ways to cope with anxiety
and stress are all important and powerful ways to grow from the
inside out.

Aside from professional help, an effective on-the-job tool is to
determine what you can take on and what you can't, and delegating certain tasks to others when you need to. If we want to truly
get to the next level, we have to stop being career martyrs and
seek help from those around us. Get to know what tasks your
colleagues are doing and those a few rungs under you. Are work
responsibilities evenly distributed? Are you getting the help you
need with the tasks you need to get done? If not, schedule some
time with your supervisor and have a candid conversation about
what you're taking on and where you could use support. You're
not helping anyone if your growing to-do list is pushing you to
the brink of burnout. The key here is to be clear about your ask
and focus on the business's end goals. It's not personal; it's about
streamlining and being as efficient as possible at getting the best
product out there—sometimes, you just can't go it alone.

Next, practice more empathy with yourself. I slowly began to replace thoughts that led me to believe something was "wrong" with me, those that were rooted in judgment, with thoughts that allowed me to feel my emotions, make space for them, and understand why they were there. I was also able to perceive my own reality a bit more clearly when I realized my MO was a reaction to someone else's expectations of me. I began to have more awareness of those moments when I was spreading myself thin and playing up the model minority card instead of actively creating my own goals.

So many professional women find that the way they react to others is holding them back. They're people pleasers, or women of color who have had to deal with feeling othered, or insecurities that prevent them from asserting themselves more effectively at work. Turning reactivity into assertiveness is a powerful shift in mindset. We're used to being reactive because it gives us a better sense of how to navigate the world safely. And because we've been doing it for so long, maybe even our whole lives, it's not necessarily something we are aware of. Until we get to the point of feeling stuck, unhappy, and frustrated. Other people's energy or reactions—particularly in a professional setting—can also easily have the power to derail us. Ultimately the cost in these scenarios falls on the employee suffering through this emotional labor. We can become discouraged and train ourselves to quiet our voices, feeling helpless to make a difference. Just like the bottling up of our own feelings, the amount of emotional resources needed to deal with microaggressions can also cause us to burn out.

When we are constantly focused on following orders and reacting to our environment, we lose out on the precious time needed to create the space for us to proactively assert our leadership skills as a natural next step in the career ladder we are so fervently climbing.

No matter where you are on your career ladder, practice telling others what you need and setting boundaries. This may not come naturally, I know. Many of us are so used to feeling like we need to take care of everyone and anyone at the expense of our own needs that actually expressing what we need and setting boundaries at times doesn't even cross our minds. But now it's time to set schedules, strategize what hours are off-limits for work, and draw some lines around our time and energy. And, most important, when we feel like we're being taken advantage of or we're not getting back the value we're putting into the work and professional relationships around us, we have to get used to saying no. "No, I can't take on another project this week." "Thank you for considering me, but no, I'm not available." "At this time, I only have the bandwidth to take on paid projects. Thank you for thinking of me."

We can also bring more mental clarity to our day-to-day lives by practicing being more direct about what we need to do our best work. For example, how many times do you ask permission in a normal day instead of proactively standing up for what you want and how you want it? "May I add a thought here?" "Could I try seeing if doing it *this* way will work?" "Maybe we can aim to start executing this next week?"

If this rings a bell, then consider replacing these doubt-laden questions with more straight-to-the-point statements: "My thought is this…" "Doing it this way will mean X, Y, Z…" "Let's start executing next week. Does anyone need more time?" When you don't need to ask, don't do it. It's a small step you can use to start shifting from being more reactive to being more assertive. (I'll get more into advocating for yourself later.) Start exercising your voice by speaking out and being more direct with boundaries around your time and energy.

And last but not least, embrace self-care practices. Part of what kept me sane while I was cooped up working from home during the height of the pandemic was finally checking in with myself on a daily basis. That thing everyone talks about, "self-care"—a concept that my parents never practiced, let alone taught me—struck a meaningful chord in my life. It's meant making a habit of tuning into my own needs before reacting to the demands of others, and knowing that taking care of myself helps me show up with more intention and purpose.

For me, practicing self-care on a small scale means daily intentional routines around meditation, movement, and sitting down for meals without distractions. It also means doing a deep cleaning of relationships that have become one-sided or unnecessarily draining, and replacing guilt with gratitude toward myself. I take pride in what I do, but I also know that it's not all of me. This new mentality helps put equal value on other roles in my life so that I'm not so fixated on finding self-worth just in my career. I don't have it completely assimilated yet, but I'm a proud work in progress.

Those moments when I find myself overcompensating or hooked on the adrenaline rush are now thankfully few and far between, because I've learned how to identify that voice that eventually leads me straight into exhaustion. It's a thin line, because, of course, we can get real fulfillment from our jobs. I certainly do; it gives me purpose, and it feels like I'm doing something that at my core I was meant to do. But it's also important to bring balance. To make sure I'm also allowing myself, as a human, to grow and be other things, such as a thoughtful daughter, a good friend, and, down the road, someone who makes space and time for a family of my own, without feeling like I have to choose between my work identity and my family life. I'm laying that healthy groundwork now. The truth is, it only gets more demanding from here.

Growth is uncomfortable because it requires something new from us, an unknown that we may have to learn from scratch. When we live in this constant sense of survival, dismissing the burnout that's loudly knocking at our door, it can easily make us lose sight of ourselves and our purpose. By addressing this, taking care of our mental health, and making self-care a priority, we're able to focus on a bigger picture and start truly showing up for ourselves, defining and leaping toward our next goals with the clear minds we need to get there.

8

Repeat After Me: "My *Why* Is My Power"

As you advance in your career, maneuvering through the highs and lows of the daily grind, you might also come across frustration and the feeling of inertia—possibly similar to the feelings that led to my mini breakdown in Midtown when I realized I had lost my sense of direction. In that moment, I didn't really know how to articulate what was happening, but now I've been able to identify that a big part of the reason I reached that breaking point was because I didn't have a clear hold on my *why* and was caught up in the ebb and flow of my everyday work. After years of going a million miles an hour, I was forced by self-doubt to stand totally still, questioning my every action like I was walking on eggshells. Like most people who have constantly focused on surviving, striving, and proving themselves, it can be hard to see the forest for the trees. *What is the purpose of all this? Am I where I'm supposed to be?*

Our *why* is our sense of purpose, mission, passion—that thing that at our core makes us feel like we're working toward something worthwhile and intentional. It can act as the foundation that holds us up when the going gets tough, when we get in our own way, or when uncontrollable outside factors play a role in pushing us off-balance.

Gaining a better understanding of that thing that reinforces what's at the end of the tunnel will not only give your drive a better sense of direction, but it can also serve as your anchor when you feel stuck or discouraged, fall offtrack, or become doubtful. It can help counteract the triggers that come from a lifetime of reacting to your environment or from having grown up in a household where survival mode and living in the shadows was a way of life.

In the beginning stages of your career, your *why* may not be too clear, and that's fine. You might feel pressure to pursue that one thing you're "meant to do"—but that can be unrealistic and counterproductive. When we fixate on the singularity of a divine calling, we may miss out on valuable lessons of growth, resilience, and discovery along the way.

I wasn't looking for that one thing, that one passion, at first. I was more concerned about learning anything and everything that gave me an opportunity to understand the dos and don'ts of the professional world. My undocumented status didn't exactly give me my pick of any dream job. But it did condition me to make every experience count, even if a given professional opportunity wasn't directly connected to what I ultimately wanted to do, and it helped me stay optimistic when I didn't know if my efforts would pay off.

In my Mary Kay days, one of the main ways I was able to

move product was through parties that involved getting a group of women together (strangers or repeat customers) and offering them free makeovers in their homes. These were essentially makeup tutorials and try-ons, during which I injected product knowledge and prepared them for the final sale at the end of our time together. Finding leads or hosts who would share the opportunity with friends and family was key to my business. Initially my go-to was tapping into my list of recurring clientele. The problem was that my network was as small as my hometown. If I was really going to be able to make enough money to finish college, I knew I had to go beyond the few family and friends who would buy the occasional item. In order to grow, I had to get the products in front of more women and venture out to nearby cities.

So I had to get creative. I took it old-school, picked up the phonebook (yeah, that thing), randomly opened up pages, and went down the list of numbers, cold-calling strangers.

"Hi, Mary Ann, my name is Daniela. I'm a Mary Kay consultant, and I'm reaching out to you because a friend who wanted to remain anonymous [a lie—I totally just landed on your name in the phonebook] had the opportunity to pick one lucky person to gift a beauty makeover to [technically true], and she chose you! Congratulations! [Never underestimate the power of flattery.] As a courtesy, you can invite up to five friends to join. [Please take this shot-in-the-dark attempt at growing my business seriously.]" Then I'd hold my breath.

There was a mixed bag of responses, repetitions of some version of the following: a click and a dead line, a "No, thank you," and, after what felt like an endless train of rejections, the holy grail, "That's so thoughtful. I'd love that." At the sound of this response, I'd quickly snap into action and schedule them on the spot to fill up my calendar. Not all parties were a success. Some were canceled, and some didn't amount to many sales. But now I realize that the experience I gained was priceless and really helped hone my voice and resilience to rejection.

After getting over the stage fright, I set aside my feelings and insecurities, and roused myself to stare rejection right in the eye. This whole shtick of looking for new clients in the phonebook was entirely something of my imagination—or perhaps my desperation—that I saw as a building block toward developing my career. No one was holding me accountable or laying down the ground rules. And having that *why*—consciously creating opportunities to build the path for it—made it more bearable to hear those nos and get good at consistently deflecting them. We can acknowledge those moments of feeling defeated, rejected, or dismissed without letting them consume us, if we can learn not to take them personally. One way to do this is consistency of action in putting ourselves out there and reframing what "no" actually means; instead of hearing it as an absolute, it can be an invitation to try again. I trained to hear it as a "not right now" instead of a "never." And that, in turn, taught me the power of shifting and being flexible about following up by trying something different.

Getting used to putting yourself out there and being open to nos can help you get over your fear of all the connotations of what that no might mean. It can feel easier to lean in to inaction to shield us from the fear of the what-ifs: *What if they think I'm a joke? What if they don't take me seriously? What if they judge me?*

What if I don't do well? They build up into a massive wall that keeps us from fully developing and realizing our *why*, keeping us in the shadow of doubt and taking away the power we actually have to make the changes we want in our life. Eventually, when we put ourselves out there enough, uncomfortably sitting in the ambiguity of potential rejection, we learn that it isn't personal.

How can we uncover our purpose—or know what it is, for that matter—if we haven't been through the sort of experience that rattles us, seeding doubt in our very ability to create and develop that purpose in the first place? If it feels hard but you still get that little rush of adrenaline thinking about the impact you'll make in your own life or the lives of others, you're onto something. Those moments of discomfort were important building blocks toward making room for my bigger *why*. They can act as data points to move forward in the right direction, our "aha moments." Having that clear focus of why I needed that experience made it easier to cut off the noise of all the uncertainty swirling around me brought about because of my legal status.

On your way to develop your purpose, you'll find that what we may view as failure or resistance is not something we can avoid, and that instead of standing down and walking away from it, we can try walking through it. If you put in that hard work, stay open to the different iterations of work opportunities your purpose may take you to, and lean into putting yourself outside of your comfort zone, the reward is self-knowledge. It helps us understand ourselves better and uncover what's really important to us. Think of those experiences that test you as strengthening your inner knowing—your gut feeling. It's that internal compass that's going to be valuable and needed to craft our career with more creativity, purpose, and confidence.

I pictured my dream outcome on my way to Mary Kay parties: booking my one-way ticket to New York, sitting in an office, going to events and networking with other professionals in the media space who had influence and decision-making power over storytelling about our culture. I could feel myself there. I wasn't hung up on where I wanted to work or what I wanted to do in that industry—that would come later. Right then, all I wanted was to be a part of that world. I felt a sense of purpose big enough to enable many different versions of how to execute it. I listened to my gut and kept continuously building a foundation of opportunity instead of sitting back, not letting my current reality or circumstances dictate what was possible ahead, and waiting for luck to fall at my doorstep. It was a balancing act, a dance in which I couldn't necessarily predict the next step, but I knew I had to stay in it. Keep trying, even if in the moment I was doing something—like selling beauty and skin-care products in strangers' homes—that seemingly had nothing to do with what I ultimately wanted to do. Because in that process, I was learning valuable self-taught professional know-how: sales skills, speaking to strangers and getting them to warm up to me, feeling out of my league but doing the work in front of me anyway, building financial independence so I could afford my dream career. I didn't let embarrassment, rejection, or vulnerability get in the way of my goals—all skills that would come in handy when I landed my job as a booking producer. Find value in your current experience, even if you don't love it. Whether it's the way you approach your work or team, a new perspective you brought to a company or organization, or a hard skill you earned. Get creative about how you express your own work narrative.

Nowadays, what used to be a clear-cut career path for previous generations has turned into a bevy of choices and zigzags that can cause decision paralysis and inertia. We have tons of options and paths our families didn't get the luxury to have. We know that we can start in one career and pivot to the next; we can be a producer and also work to be a journalist in other ways, like in my case. We can be many things all at once or in different stages of our lives. This is exciting, and opens up paths that our family and generations before us couldn't experience for themselves, but it has also introduced a choice overload that past generations might not understand. We may be bogged down by a certain type of information fatigue. Yet we have maintained the need to find the perfect role. Every microscopic career decision starts to feel heavy: Am I making the right choice? And is this version of the right choice my own or someone else's?

For many of us, the expectations about paths we feel the pressure to take, whether they come from us or from an external source such as our own families, can feel heavy. For many minority women, particularly in immigrant communities, there's also the tug of putting their family's needs and communities first in their career decisions. We are often conditioned to take on the expectations or paths we think others have laid out or need of us. This makes our choice overload, and the possibility of pursuing our own passions, even more complicated. When we take the time to dig for our *why*, it often gives us the focus we need to take the best next step forward and not worry about the perfect one.

This is an issue a friend of mine, whom I met at an alumni

award ceremony, struggled with. Anushay is bright, successful, and a go-getter. She grew up in the United States and in Syria, and studied international conflict in college. She developed a passion for working with refugees to amplify their voices by humanizing the refugee experience, to advance humanitarian and policy agendas by advocating for the protection and safe resettlement of families, and to educate others on the troubles of resettlement and the cultural nuances that come with all of this. She has won numerous awards and recognition for her work in this space, and even worked on a project with a presidential candidate on outreach to immigrant communities.

Yet, despite all this outstanding experience, she felt stuck in her career, unable to find her next step. She'd constantly find herself in a loop of anxiety, asking herself, *Who am I doing it for? Society? My community? Internalized pressure based on harboring (inter)generational trauma and sacrifice? Am I doing enough? Is this path guaranteed?* Anushay was putting all of this pressure on herself to find that perfect fit that would check all the boxes above, and along the way she was losing a sense of just how valuable her skills were in her industry.

But she found that digging into her own sense of purpose, without being tainted by the expectations of others, allowed her to contain these types of ruminating thoughts and let her think of her career beyond the constraints of just one role.

Nonprofits always felt like a good fit for her, and she usually maintained work at those companies. When we homed in on her *why*, it was all about being a bridge builder between cultures and communities. In the end, her desire to work within international development and humanitarian emergencies was a professional aspiration, but it was also personal. Witnessing the ongoing calamities and hardships evolving in the homes of her parents and friends inspired her to create change and awareness.

By reaching the core of this *why*, Anushay expanded her career opportunities. The idea of working beyond the nonprofit space and not having to follow the traditional path she thought was expected let her broaden the ways in which she saw her career develop. It empowered her to think about her career with more autonomy and creativity, including the possibility of being her own boss. Now anything was on the table, from entertainment opportunities like consulting on the development of scripts about refugees, to social media campaigns targeting social justice issues more broadly. Understanding the overall umbrella of her purpose—her *why*—allowed her to see her career beyond just one role or one linear path. It ultimately gave her the initiative to start putting herself out there in different ways—for example, creating a personal website to publicly show the many intersections and industries her work touched and included. She took more ownership of her career instead of being fixated on the linear path she had previously concocted in her mind.

When you connect with your purpose and are able to articulate it, your options ahead widen. You no longer become attached to one organization or one role; you start to view yourself in an expansive way, with more power and autonomy over the career choices in your future. You open your eyes to the many paths toward your own success.

My *why* or passion at the beginning of my career was to be a part of a process, to get to work on a team, to have the opportunity to learn, to be of use in whatever way was required. My *why* was to find a role somewhere, anywhere, where work wasn't just for survival—like it has been for my parents. It was to make their sacrifices worth it while finding enjoyment through the challenge of the early learning curves, leaning into it all.

At the start, I had to find my way on my own. I didn't have access to mentors who would guide me along, or help define my *why*. Yet, nowadays, in the same ways there's pressure to find that one perfect, fitting purpose, or job, there also tends to be a hell of a lot of pressure to find the "right" mentor. Oftentimes this person is portrayed as the one who will guide us up some luminous stairway to success, opening magical doors, introducing us to the perfect contacts, and even advocating for our every need in the workplace. But in the real world, mentors like that are hard to come by. I've been in countless informational meetings with soon-to-be college grads who eagerly scout for potential mentors with as much focus as Greek rush week. This level of pressure to find the "perfect" mentor can become counterproductive.

Don't get me wrong. Mentors and sponsors are absolutely important and necessary. But if you're struggling to find them, I encourage you to expand how you go about building beneficial professional contacts. Instead of focusing on that *one* person and putting all of your eggs in their basket, start your very own *community* of professional allies. Developing your *why* and bringing it to life is easier when you share the journey with a community of professionals with whom you're intentional about keeping in touch, a team of badass people who are the private army of support that you turn to not just for inspiration but also for guidance and, when appropriate, for extra advocacy on your behalf. The best relationships don't just help mold you into the type of professional you want to be; they also help hold a microphone up to your skills and value in the workplace.

These relationships open the door to another key factor in developing your *why*: relationship equity. Relationship equity is a step beyond networking. It's the kind of connection you establish with people who will vouch for you when you're not in the room, because you've given them a sense of what value you bring to the table firsthand *and* because you've helped them build their own careers. These relationships become your professional allies. You check in with them often and seek counsel from them. There is value on both sides of the relationship. They don't have to be several career rungs above you. Some of the most beneficial career allies can be those you network with laterally, who are in the same trenches as you or right above you. Your career has a long runway, so nurturing and creating relationships across all levels is key.

If it's hard for you to think of solid examples of these people in your life now—for example, if you're just starting out—then I encourage you to seek inspiration, someone who makes you think, *I aspire to do that, I could do that, I admire that.* When I didn't have professional mentors early on, I learned a great deal by simply identifying traits, qualities, and skills that I admired in others. I watched my boss and boss's boss articulate their ideas, carefully observing how they carried and expressed themselves. I took note of their email style, observed their decision-making processes. These became my micro-mentoring moments. Without realizing it, these people became my professional mentors. Identifying their values and how they forged ahead was just as valuable to me as mentorship, even if they weren't directly advising or opening up spaces for me yet.

Don't wait for someone to take you under their wing as your teacher or mentor; instead, become an active student. Look to those you admire, those you'd like to work with one day, those you'd like to be someday. Study their habits and the ways they work the room. This will help you define your purpose. It will allow your *why* to surface, and it will help you shape it into what you want it to become on a professional level.

I found this person in Mika Brzezinski at my job at *Morning Joe*. I admired Mika and was eager to learn from her, but I knew I couldn't just come in with guns blazing and shout from the rooftops that I wanted her to be my mentor during the first few months on the job. Something Mika has said a dozen times during her Know Your Value conferences that has always stayed with me is this: "Respect first; friendships will follow." And it couldn't have proven to be a better piece of advice. That's exactly the path I followed with her. I found ways to navigate her world, be of value, make myself indispensable, and create a rapport, while remaining acutely aware of the nuances in her busy life.

Every mentorship relationship, no matter the hierarchy, is a two-way street. Even if you don't have much experience or are new at the job professionally, there is always something of value you can provide to the person or group guiding you. Keep your ear to the ground, listen intently, connect with what you can do to help elevate that person's work experience, and go for it. No gesture or action is too small. Remember: You are of value no matter how much or how little experience you may have.

Once I earned Mika's respect, trust soon followed, and then the invaluable opportunity to learn from her and, later on, the chance to collaborate with her professionally. Our relationship began to evolve from boss-employee to mentor-mentee, and she gradually took me under her wing.

Once, she called me to set and handed me a folded note she had written during commercial that said, "Come sit in on my meeting at noon and take notes!" Her quick scribble referred to a meeting she'd set up with the heads of a beauty brand, where they were scheduled to discuss teaming up for a partnership with her platform Know Your Value. As a junior-level employee, I couldn't really provide any value to this meeting, and Mika didn't really need me to take notes for her. Those notes were for me. She was extending an unspoken opportunity for me to learn by exposure by getting a chance to be in a decision-making room. Over time, this grew into her asking me to staff her at noteworthy events. I fed her information as needed and helped her nail every detail of those evenings. In turn, she introduced me to Fortune 500 CEOs and VIPs. It was her personal resolve to give me access and exposure to different people, and peripheral opportunities and experiences to learn from, that were invaluable to my career.

The technical advice came later in our relationship. She shared tips on how to present information when I did TV appearances, coached me on how to advocate better for myself during behind-the-scenes negotiations, and answered my calls when I had one-off career questions. She took my scrappiness and grit and gave me a chance to channel it with opportunities that I could use toward my professional growth and the development of my *why*.

In the end, I didn't always have a clear idea of the end purpose of each career step, but it made it easier to *identify* opportunities to advance in places where others might not have seen the value—like obsessing over coffee orders, which was a key stepping-stone to getting ahead in my career. Now that my career was going through a growth spurt, I began to understand that my *why* was more than just being a part of a process and having the opportunity to learn; it was about finding a way to use this newfound platform to deliver a deeper message and take on a multidimensional approach to my purpose.

Doubling down on your *why* and your own version of success takes time, and it can be especially difficult to define if your idea of success is influenced by whatever cultural or familial version of that word you've consciously or unconsciously believed to be your own. It can call for you to reject the very definitions or examples of success that seemed to work for others but that don't work as well for you. I know this may not be what you want to hear, but we need those moments when we feel like we're stuck or even struggling to get ahead in order to dig deep in ourselves and really ask ourselves about the pillars that are important for us to have in our work lives. These experiences can help deepen our self-knowledge, as I mentioned before, and it's the strongest foundation we have for a sustainable career.

Kailee, a woman in her twenties, shared with me that she had a job where being a total workaholic brought her a sense of pride. The line between her own identity and her work also felt blurred; both the wins and losses in her role felt deeply personal to her. But her world stopped when her father had to enter hospice care. The company she worked for at the time decided to let her go after seeing the amount of time she'd have to take off to be at her father's side. That caused her to reevaluate and uncover what really mattered to her—her *why*—which was: family, working at a company that valued balance, and maintaining a career that fit her sense of purpose.

As she searched for new employment, she let go of the idea that she needed a job where she'd have to work long hours and grind hard to feel validated about her worth as an employee. She looked for jobs that could complement and align with her *why*. Flexibility, balance, teamwork. Sometimes your why isn't just *what* you do but *how* you do it.

That year, she entered a new managerial job, and she started showing up to work differently. She made respect, empathy, and work-life balance part of her leadership style. She also welcomed her first baby. Instead of thriving on being a workaholic, she became strategic about how she worked and when she worked, so that she could prioritize her child. She didn't lessen the value of her work, but she was smarter about where she got her validation from. Kailee still loved what she did at work, but by focusing on her *why*, she became a better manager. Her employees admired her ability to set clear boundaries, not stay long hours, and turn off her work phone after a certain time. By understanding her *why*, she ultimately became better at her job. It gave her a deeper meaning of what a job meant to her and her identity because she consciously chose the benchmarks of what success and purpose meant to her, instead of her role at work doing that for her.

In my role as an author and journalist, telling my story crafted the next step of my career. My *why* became reporting stories about marginalized communities on TV and online, as well as sharing and creating content to empower women in different areas of life. It's what forged my unconventional path from being a behind-the-scenes producer to being in front of the camera as a full-time reporter for the same show. Yet reaching this sense of purpose took time.

When I received DACA, there was a nagging sense that I needed to reckon with that part of my identity in some way. I'd never felt like I needed to have a big coming-out moment about how I had been undocumented. But now I was living in New York City, where there was a level of acceptance and awareness without judgment on this topic that came as a relief to someone like me. This city showed me that different ethnicities, backgrounds, sexual orientations, and upbringings weren't always vilified in the ways that they were in the small town I had grown up in. New York was home to grassroots movements that helped DACA come to life, a center for exceptionally courageous activists who were without legal status themselves and told the world they were "undocumented and unafraid." They shared their truth vulnerably, before DACA was there to protect them, to make change and let others know they weren't alone in this silent fight. Bravery at its finest.

And as all of this sunk in, it suddenly hit me: I needed to do something about it too, in my own way. I felt guilt and shame over hiding my reality, even though DACA allowed me to move through the world a bit more safely. That's why, when the chance presented itself, I didn't hesitate to say yes.

While networking with other media professionals inside my company during those first few years at NBCUniversal, I reached out to an editor who oversaw Latino content for one of their news properties. At this point, I still hadn't come across many other Latino professionals. I was one of the few, and I was eager to begin growing my community of professional allies. Sandra, an incredibly kind and wonderful editorial director, agreed to an in-person informational meeting of sorts. It was there, between small talk and conversation over editorial coverage, that I found myself telling her my backstory, what it was like to be a DACA recipient, and the struggles I'd had to face to simply get my foot in the door. It was the first time I had opened up to anyone in a professional setting about this. And to be honest, it felt quite liberating.

After listening to me attentively, she said, "You should write about it." She was the first person who made me realize my experience was worth sharing and that my voice was important. And even more so, she was the first one to give me a space and a platform to do it.

It was my chance to make a difference now, and I jumped on it. I sat in front of my computer, a little nervous but also feeling empowered by this opportunity. I had written about my story before for college essays and had spent hours developing short stories around my experience—a self-soothing outlet that helped me deal with the anxiety caused by my circumstances—but I had never done it for an audience of anything close to the reach of this nationally known news outlet.

Once the ideas were on the page, I set out to pick my words with close discernment, making sure I was as transparent and raw as I could be to reflect what felt like a big coming-out moment. Still somewhat hesitant, I sent her a rough draft, and soon after, my first-person piece was posted on NBCLatino.com.

I was swimming in a mixed bag of emotions: excited, empowered, and extremely vulnerable. Being so naked with my story in front of strangers was disquieting. The unease even made me hesitant to share the link with my own circle. But surely it was all worth it; this act of bravery had to amount to something. I stared at the page, waiting for the comments to come pouring in, the feedback on my big making-a-difference debut, and then...nothing. No ticker tape parade for my great moment of courage. Alas, the world just kept on turning! Sure, it was newsworthy enough to get published—it happened to be a DACA anniversary—but the reality was that there was nothing extraordinary about my story. In the grand scheme of things, I was one of almost a million DACA recipients in this country. People who were in my situation and read the piece likely felt that my words resonated with them and maybe even felt less alone, but nothing in my career dramatically shifted.

Although this piece didn't make any waves on a big news scale—not even a ripple—it was nevertheless a mini personal turning point in my life. Having to sit down and analyze my situation and what it meant in my life to be undocumented, writing it all down and putting it out there through a published post, was the first real step I took to reclaim my narrative and define my *why*. An invisible weight had been lifted, and suddenly I could breathe a little easier when speaking about it.

I told my story in part to help others understand our internal fight and resilience as immigrants, because I believe every story of resilience serves a larger cause. But in all honesty, there was a part of me that also did it for myself. Because I, too, needed to see those words in writing. I needed to read them out loud and remind myself that my circumstances and struggles didn't define me. What I discovered is that in taking up space, whether it's in our careers or in our lives, we have to free ourselves from internal self-limiting beliefs that have turned into shackles, locked in place by our circumstances. We can't let them define us.

You hold the power to create the next chapters you want and deserve.

For years, I worked on being the person at my job known for turning a no into a yes, being dogged about chasing hard-to-get guests for months or even years, working around the clock to pursue the strongest voices for the top news stories, and all the other things that my job required of me. And I was doing fine. The feedback I was given on my work performance was always good.

But after a while, I felt like there were other parts of me that I wasn't fully attending to, and they were starting to fizzle out. Something was missing. Everything was so one-sided, so boxed in, so linear. Like I was being forced to fracture parts of myself because I was convinced that seeking opportunities outside of hard news would contradict how my colleagues viewed me. I needed to find a way to reignite and feed my other interests and passions, those that made me feel whole. I realized that I love engaging my creativity to help women become empowered, whether it's through sharing resources or through writing about issues like career development, financial wellness, or mental health. I also love my role as a storyteller, and I knew that cultivating these passions was essential to my *why*. I had to find a way to make this happen and battle my inherent inclination to shut down the parts of me that didn't fit in the box I had created for myself in terms of how my career should look.

At first it was terrifying. I feared that if I worked on other things I was passionate about on the side—like writing about women entrepreneurs, financial health, career, self-worth, and so on—I would no longer be taken seriously by my colleagues at my booking job. And God knows I cared too much about what people thought, especially in a professional setting, to really listen to that inner voice that was begging me to develop in new ways. That internal push and pull took a toll. It was the Daniela who wanted to live authentically by doing the things that energized me—storytelling, hosting interviews, continuing to share with other women through writing—versus the Daniela who wanted to continue climbing the standard corporate ladder.

It terrified me, because there wasn't a box for this. Since these goals didn't fit a preexisting role and went beyond my job requirements, I feared the judgment I could receive for drawing outside the lines. The contradiction I'd cause in people's minds. Even when I couldn't pinpoint where and who the judgment would come from, I imagined the worst. It took me a while—time I spent drained, unhappy, and a bit disillusioned—to realize that by fighting this urge to evolve, I was working against my ability to show up fully. There I was following some unwritten rule on building a *safe* and linear career instead of writing my own rules toward a career that was truly fulfilling. When I finally understood this, it gave me a new sense of freedom. Now the challenge wasn't about overcoming adversity; it was about expanding my thinking about who I was. I had to start giving myself the necessary space to develop my interests and my *why* in new ways.

Our purpose is what drives us to push through our discomfort and reach our goals. It calls for us to get to know ourselves. It calls for us to embrace our different layers and multidimensionality.

I wish someone had told me what I now know deep in my bones to be true: *You are allowed to be multidimensional, damn it!* I turned that into my motto. Still, I rationalized it intellectually and had to work harder than ever to find the courage to actually put my own thoughts into action. Part of me feared realizing the power my own multidimensionality held for me. It was just waiting for me to step into it.

True fulfillment sometimes calls us to be brave enough to draw outside the lines. You are allowed to have different pursuits than what's expected of you. Your path, passions, and purpose don't have to make sense to anyone else but you. Don't wait for permission or feel that your only option is to follow the current path. If you're someone who wants to transcend the norm and make career moves that might be atypical, don't wait for a playbook for that. You're not going to find it, because it hasn't been written yet. Instead, turn inward and ask yourself: *What do I need to work on internally to give myself permission to step into my multidimensionality?*

Once I gave myself permission to tap into that multidimensionality, I allowed myself to nurture other interests without anticipating what others may think, and this, in turn, actually added extra value to my own role at work. I began to share content and resources across different divisions (both on-air and online) with minimal support, which also served as a springboard to assume more responsibility and explore new opportunities while still being taken seriously at work. I started tapping into the communities of professional allies I had been growing, building my confidence, and honing my voice. In essence, I was deepening that self-trust and relationship with myself so that I could better engage in creating meaningful work that would impact others.

As I continue to work on myself and develop these other parts of me, I've learned to embrace my otherness even more. It's okay to not check off all the standard boxes. It's okay to be multidimensional. It's okay to not belong and to be unique. Just like you have the power to create your own story, you can also create your own unique spaces in your career. You don't need to fit into a lane; you can make a new one.

My friend Mariana, who is an entrepreneur and total boss, has a corporate job and created her own accessories line on the side during the pandemic. When we chatted about what her *why* was, she explained that, sure, she loved seeing her designs on other people and seeing how it made them feel about themselves, but the real drive? "Money!" she blurted out. "I want to make lots of it! I want to be financially independent." She was unabashed about saying what many of us are thinking. This was really important to her, and she owned that.

Even if your purpose isn't the cookie-cutter one you feel is expected of you, you need to be honest with yourself and others. Your goals don't have to look a certain way to be powerful and meaningful. Your *why* is never going to be the same as someone else's, and so what? It doesn't make you or them better. For Mariana, money doesn't just mean living a comfortable lifestyle; it's also about being able to be at ease with her work enough to enjoy being a creative, to be able to balance work with other parts of her life because she's not worried about living paycheck to paycheck. Her *why* is enjoying life and having time to enjoy it with others, and for her, that looks like money!

I happen to be a person for whom the nature of my work is deeply embedded in my life's mission, much like Anushay. For others, like Kailee, that mission can be taking care of their families and fostering a career where work-life balance takes the lead, while for people like Mariana, it might mean being able to freely order the extra guac on your chips. Go ahead and make this personal to you. It's what will drive you forward.

What's more, the *whys* in our lives are not stagnant. They're ever-evolving and malleable. We're not robots. Career indecision and reboots happen as we grow. Don't beat yourself up about that. We are worthy of developing our joy too, and that means there may be different variations of our *why* that we want to explore further.

Break free from the notion that you have to fit in one role and stick to one lane. The more you show up as your full self and bring your unique sense of *why* to work, the more beneficial it is not only for you but also for everyone around you. The best work ahead of us uses that intersection of different identities we hold, which serves as an anchor for our purpose. We have innate richness just because of the fact that we are many things, and our duality is the best thing we can own.

Being involved in many things and working hard in different lanes, not just in news, has made me better at my news job. It has given me the confidence and courage to show up more authentically because I've built a community around my work—and outside of it—based on the shared value of empowering women, communities of color, and immigrants. Digging into that fact made me see myself beyond just one role or job. I can now show up with more layers of knowledge, context, and lived experience. I can tap into my multidimensionality in a real way. It's taken me a few years to find this flow. That's why it's important to set the right foundation for success in a way that works for *you* rather than try to pressure yourself to follow someone else's path.

Identify what work values are important to you, what drains you, and what uplifts you. Maybe you are laser-focused on moving up the ladder, getting to the C-suite, or branching out on your own. Maybe the idea of endless side projects sucks the life out of you. Maybe you're compelled to find a platform to share your creativity. No matter your path, you've got to make that trajectory yours and yours alone. It's up to you to remain aware of your path and make the necessary shifts to continue following what gives you a sense of purpose and peace. This will help you set up your career to confidently take up space and take it to the next level.

Move consciously toward your goals as if they're within reach, despite what or who might stand in your way. Forget the reaction or inaction of others. You have to become emboldened by your own dreams, see your own potential, and recognize your discipline, your perseverance, and all of the dogged, tireless work you've endured to get here. Block out the noise, expectations, rulebooks (really there are none!). The path is yours to define; you have to lean into it and own it (no one will do this for you) and embrace its multidimensionality and ebbs and flows. And when you finally arrive at the destination you envisioned, the one that you have rightfully earned, speak up and own it.

9

Grab a Seat and Order Coffee Too

O nce you get a seat at the table and start navigating corporate culture or the workplace at large, it's time to start learning how to effectively advocate for yourself and "work the table"— that is, find your voice and use it with confidence.

Speaking up and advocating for ourselves is easier said than done. It can be more comfortable to choose silence. *Will they think I'm too bossy? Too direct? Ungrateful?* But sometimes the stakes for a potential career-changing conversation are just too high to keep quiet. It came to a head for me in 2016.

Morning Joe was on the road in South Carolina, covering the presidential election. Since it was a traveling show, only a handful of the usual morning-show team were asked to join, and due to my booking skills, hands-on set knowledge, and previous on-the-road experience with the team, this included me. That morning, our show was scheduled to take place in the lobby of a historic hotel in downtown Charleston with a live audience. Lucky for me, the commute was only an elevator ride away, a rarity of convenience.

I was downstairs by four a.m., prepping the local runners I had scouted to help coordinate the entrance of our audience, meeting with security to go over protocol, giving marching orders for the all-important coffee run for our on-air talent, tracking guest logistics, reviewing necessary editorial materials for the show—I reveled in that nonstop action. My second cup of coffee started to kick in by eight a.m. We were on a commercial break when Mika signaled me over to the set and told me her chief of staff had fallen sick, so she needed me to go with her to Tennessee that afternoon, where she was due to deliver a speech at a women's conference.

The crowd filling up the lobby behind our set roared in applause as our hosts closed the show, right on the heels of nine in the morning. My eyes traced the open path our security officer had created, leading the way for Mika and me. Our movements were swift and intentional, going from the hotel lobby door straight to the SUV to avoid the swarm of fans that would inevitably stop and ask for photos. We were on a strict schedule, and my ability to do my job well now rested on getting in and out of places efficiently and on time without meandering while keeping Mika at ease and prepped along the way.

As we sat in the SUV on the way to the airport, it dawned on me that this was the first time she and I were alone together, one-on-one. *If I'm ever going to make an impression on her about who I am other than the scrappy and efficient show coordinator, it's now,* I thought. I was sure I had earned her trust, and I wanted her to know the added value I could bring if I was given the opportunity. This was my chance to pitch it to her. It was now or never.

But what do I say?

I could feel myself overthinking, psyching myself out, and that triggered the dreaded fight-or-flight physical reaction: shoulders tensed, stomach churning, jaw clenched, heart racing. But all of this was replaced by thoughts of the situations I had observed firsthand growing up—which I'm sure many of you observed as well—in which people made themselves indispensable yet were too humble to ask for more. I thought about the women in my family; had they been in my shoes, they would have felt like the level of support and value they gave their bosses or supervisors was more than enough. Like they said to me with the best of intentions, "You just worry about doing your job well, and they'll speak up for you when the time is right." They were unaware that this piece of advice wouldn't fly in the type of corporate America I was navigating. They thought that hard work and gratitude alone would pave the way for their *our time has come* moment.

But my experience coming up in this world told me to know better and ask myself, *How, when, and why will my time come?* I wasn't about to leave it to chance or to other people's whims. Generationally, the family precedent was to opt for the safer, quieter, humbler work self. I knew I had to act differently. No one hears your wants and needs louder than you do. It was a tough realization to come to terms with, because it meant pinpointing the shortcomings of the incredibly strong women who raised me. I knew I had to articulate my value better than my family had and actively speak out for my ideas. Because if you don't use your voice, no one will know what you want, what you're capable of.

The consequences of not speaking up suddenly felt scarier than
the nerves I had in the moment. And just like that, I regained
control of myself, my words, my body. I rolled my shoulders back,
took deep breaths to release the knots in my stomach, and dared
to say the things that I had wanted to say for a while but hadn't
found the right moment to do so.

"Can I get your opinion on something I've been thinking
of?" I asked Mika as we drove down the highway.

She looked up from her phone and turned to me, and my
heart skipped a beat when I realized I had her full attention,
probably for the first time ever. All our interactions before then
had had to do with some task or errand, confirming logistics or
verifying editorial information or checking off other to-do list
items. Now I had the floor, and I was going to talk about...
myself?! I gulped, uncomfortable with the undivided attention.

Is it too late to change my mind now?

No, this was my now-or-never moment, and I wasn't about
to screw it up. So I took a deep breath, looked her straight in
the eye, and carefully articulated how much I admired the platform she had built to help women, citing the specifics of how I'd
witnessed the impact her message had on women. Note: When
making a pitch or ask, bring data to what you're articulating. In
my case, it helped to show I had read up on the particulars of her
platform. Show that you did your research!

Then I added, "I'd love to get your advice on this idea I have
about a possible platform I'd like to create for young women who,
like me, struggled to get their foot in the door." Hoping that I
was striking the right tone to pique her interest, I kept going:
"It would be a space where women can find resources and tools

to open up doors in the beginning of their careers, for minority women, people of color, or Latinas like me who want mentors to learn from: Access!" *All of a sudden, I've given it a name?!* I tried to slow my racing mind before I nose-dived into total word-vomit mode. Although I didn't necessarily know how this would play out, I forced myself to keep going.

Just the thought of sticking your neck out before you feel ready can be terrifying, I know, but if you have a grip on the subject matter, go for it. Men do this all the time with more ease; meanwhile, we women tend to get hung up on the details of how we'll deliver an idea and how we'll be perceived.

Yet, sometimes, presenting an open-ended idea to a higher-up gives them an opportunity to connect with you too. You may be surprised to see where it goes. Worst-case scenario, Mika would drop some real talk about me not being ready or just show no interest; best case, she'd give me some good advice, or even want to collaborate with me in some way. If nothing at all came from this conversation, I'd still be a winner, because now she knew what I was passionate about and I could hope that she'd have me in mind for certain projects.

My mom's voice in the back of my head kept nagging me, though: "¡Baja las revoluciones!" (Slow down!) I tried to pace my cadence, enunciating my words as I moved along. Mika seemed genuinely interested.

And that's when she hit me with the question that changed our relationship from then on: "Why?"

"Because it was my own struggle."

Her one-word question opened the door for me to share the CliffsNotes version of my journey and how I got to where I was that day. I had never found my story of working to get a leg up in life remarkable—it just felt like what I had to do to build equity—but Mika found it compelling. It was the first time we connected on an emotional level; there was heart to my story, and I suspect she related it to her own family's immigrant background. I explained how I got my foot in the door regardless of my circumstances, how I hopped on that Greyhound bus on a round-trip ticket to New York City, acting like a local, landing two summer internships, all while being undocumented. And that's when she went quiet and stared out the window.

Once we arrived at the women's conference in Tennessee, I took my seat in the front row, next to a senator with whom I made small talk as we waited for Mika to take the stage. And then, in a blink, we were on a plane and landing back in Charleston.

Suddenly, the exhaustion of the day hit us both. When we made it to the hotel, we quietly walked back to our rooms to catch what little sleep we could before the next morning's live show. Even if nothing bigger came from that car-ride conversation to the airport, it had allowed me to continue to define myself on my terms, own my narrative, and use my voice. I was left with a newfound focus and a rush of empowerment about what I could do next. As the adrenaline high of that day wore off, I drifted off to sleep.

A few months went by, and on the first day of 2017, Mika FaceTimed me. Confused by the early call, I answered with matted hair and the thick, dark-rimmed glasses I didn't let *anyone* see me in. I looked a mess. Exactly what you'd expect the morning after a New Year's celebration. I hoped she could still recognize me.

"Hi, Mika. It's me, Daniela!" I said for good measure. Awkwardly.

"We're doing it," she said with excited determination. "We're making Access happen. It's going to be a book. You and I are writing it. It's going to be based on your story..."

I stared back, blinking.

Is this really happening?

Yes. As awestruck as I was in the moment, I was not surprised. This was the type of access Mika had provided from my first month on the job, when she told me I'd be going with her to a coveted New York Fashion Week show an hour before it started, or when she'd pull me into important pitch meetings for Know Your Value with heads of Fortune 500 companies. But this...this was different. I wasn't just going to be sitting or listening in; I was going to become her *collaborator*!

It required me to find my voice and do it quickly.

The first thought that crossed my mind was *Am I qualified for this?* I was still in my early twenties and not sure if I had enough experience to share in book form. But the one question that didn't come up was *Am I ready for this?* Because even though I had never written a book or done anything else along those lines, it was now clear that my story was valuable because I understood the struggle of the would-be reader to the core.

Mika had now become a sponsor who opened up doors in my career I'd never thought possible. And it all began with getting out of my comfort zone, taking a leap, chasing that rare opportunity, making room for bigger thinking. It happened because I spoke up. Yet I hadn't come to her with a business model or a fully fleshed-out plan—not even close. I had identified an opportunity to connect beyond a well-prepared pitch, and I had opened the door for an emotional connection related to the work we were individually passionate about—helping other women succeed in the workplace. It helped to have an understanding and the details of the work she was doing with her platform to better translate how I saw myself as an added asset to that work.

More important, I could see that our *whys* overlapped. There was real synergy between the types of work we were individually passionate about. I connected the dots between who I was and the work I wanted to do, and I approached it with a focus she was receptive to: bringing her message to women whose struggle I uniquely had firsthand experience with. And, equally important, I had already built trust at the show by making myself valuable to my boss (starting with getting that coffee just right!), which earned her respect enough to get her to listen to my idea. Building that trust was essential. Above all, we connected on a human level over a shared interest.

Sometimes that emotional connection can be hard to create, especially if you're working in tough environments. That's why it's important to get a good read on your environment and understand where you fall. You can also look to make lateral connections outside of your current role or across departments, not just with your supervisor or direct higher-ups. It's not about changing ourselves but about working smart and learning to share our ideas and messages in a way that others can receive and relate to. Building that rapport.

There are a few ways to do this. First, ask questions of the person you're trying to connect with. *How long have you been doing this? What drives you? How did you end up in this role?* Another tactic is to learn their professional style and their preferences on when and how they like to be communicated with. What is the best time of day for you to share an idea? Do they prefer thorough explanations over bullet points? Phone calls, texts, or emails? Also helpful is creating deeper connections by remembering details and bringing them up again; maybe they've gone on a trip recently, or had a sick family member.

Once you've created a connection or your own strategic, effective plan to communicate with decision-makers and higher-ups, it's time to ask yourself an essential question: *What value do I bring that is uniquely mine to offer?* It's not about walking through the door thinking you're going to disrupt the industry from day one with all of your creative ideas. It's about building value and seeing where your creativity could work best so that you can effectively become your own best advocate. Rarely will someone hold us by the hand and say, "It's time to get you promoted!" "Gee, you deserve more money. Let's have a conversation about your pay!" Nope. Not gonna happen. You've got to speak up and be ready to connect the dots of where you're going and the work you've put in to get there.

Say what you need to say, even if your voice feels shaky. Advocating for yourself has as much to do with what you say and do at a meeting, negotiating table, or performance review as it does with how you show up every day at work. Consider your personality and work style, and play up your strengths and unique point of view. It's time to reassess and press reset to create a way of being that is entirely more *you*—more authentic, more complete—and shows others how indispensable you are.

Mika and I wrote this piece of advice for our book *Earn It!*, and I think it's worth repeating: Don't assume everything you do will be noticed. And that's exactly what I did when I gathered the courage to share more about my *why* and my story. Sometimes you have to let others know what they might not know about you—the extra effort you're putting in, your department's success, how your individual contribution has helped move forward a project or the company bottom line, what you're passionate about within the realm of your career. Whatever it is, don't assume other people know. Especially if you're like me, constantly doing work in silos, sometimes across departments. You've got to be ready to articulate the value you've provided and the work you've done, because more often than not, no one is keeping tabs on your every move. This can be as easy as writing down your work, categorizing it, putting metrics behind it, and sharing it with others in conversation. Don't wait until you're in the negotiating room to let others know about the value you're bringing.

Practice being your own advocate. "Find your moments with the people at your company to point out what you're doing, without feeling weird about it," Mika said to me once. I don't have a problem doing that now, but it took me a long time to get there, to express myself with confidence. That's when those lists of metrics, hours, projects you keep to yourself matter. You become more emboldened to make your ask when you remind yourself of the constant work and effort you're putting forth and your goals and purpose. I bet if you make that list now, you'll be surprised by how much you've done. It's not just about celebrating your wins but also about using them as fuel for what you're advocating for.

Getting used to talking about yourself and being able to

clearly articulate what you've done so far and how you've executed it can feel brand-new, especially when you're not used to it, but it is a game changer. When speaking to your bosses and career gatekeepers, get your point across clearly. One of the things I learned from the people who are excellent at being heard and respected is that they have an ability to *articulate effectively* their ask or need. They keep it direct, concise, and to the point.

What are you asking for? Why? What are the supporting points? Don't give anyone a chance to misrepresent your needs or make assumptions. When you feel bias creep in, fight subjectivity with objectivity by clearly showing others your value from the get-go. One of the exercises I find useful is to take a moment to think about specific adjectives you want others to know you by: Straightforward? Empathetic? Pragmatic? Assertive? How do you want others to feel when you walk into or leave a room? This is an exercise I use with members of my mentorship community because feeling othered in the workplace sometimes means not being able to be seen in the way you intend, for the many reasons we've hashed out in this book already. Being intentional about exactly how you want to be seen and then taking very specific actions to build those connotations in other people's minds helps control your narrative and how others perceive you.

Ever notice how we identify leaders in the room simply by how they introduce themselves? The way we tell others what we do and how we do it says a lot about ourselves. The more we can express ourselves with confidence, assertion, and *clarity*, the more we can establish our presence and control the messaging we want for ourselves, a much-needed skill when it comes to advocating for advances in our careers. Yet how many times do we meet people and introduce ourselves, and then think, *Damn, that's not what I wanted to say. I should've said it differently. Was I clear? Did they get me?* How many networking opportunities with professionals have we missed because we weren't able to resonate with them and say what we wanted to say about ourselves clearly? Remember Estefania and how it took her a full hour to share that she was actually the founder and CEO of the company where she worked?

Having a go-to personal statement helps define your value, especially when you're meeting someone for the first time. It lets people know what you're all about and what you uniquely bring to the table, and it takes the guesswork out of the equation when nerves might get the better of you. To develop and articulate your personal statement, it's helpful to focus on first answering these four questions: *What* do you do? *Who* do you do it for? *How* do you do it? *What* have you been able to accomplish because of it?

Once you have your answers, keep in tune with your surroundings. Your personal statement is meant to work in a professional or casual setting, anything from a dinner party to a networking event or a meet-and-greet (never miss an opportunity to network!). It should be clear, concise, and somewhat casual. It could sound something like this: "My name is Daniela Pierre-Bravo, and in addition to my producing role at NBCUniversal, I am a contributor to NBC's Know Your Value. I strategize and produce content [use strong action words here!] for our website and social channels that helps marginalized women feel empowered to know and grow their value and become better advocates."

Because a good conversation is always a two-way street, you want to give the other person enough information to be clear but you also want to be concise enough not to bog them down in the details right away (hello, short attention spans!). I would follow up my own statement with something like, "I do this by booking, producing, and conducting interviews with Fortune 500 CEOs, women entrepreneurs, entertainers, and political figures." It's important to have different variations depending on your audience. This also allows someone to ask you follow-up questions, which let you get even more specific.

It's essential to actually practice the message you want to send. As you practice your personal statement, focus on all the physical tools that go hand in hand with saying it out loud: body language, posture, eye contact, and your voice itself—the way it sounds, the tonality of it, but also the words you use and even the words you don't use. Find someone to practice this with—it could be a friend, a family member, a partner—and ask them for feedback. Record yourself and then watch it. You might find that the first or second time you take a stab at it might not be how you want to sound, but that's why practice makes perfect!

As we get comfortable using our voice and speaking more confidently and directly about ourselves and our value, we still may face frustrating bits of stereotypes that continue to happen in tandem with our career growth and development, especially as women of color. Although there has been a great deal of progress, exhibiting qualities of self-assuredness and assertiveness can still be interpreted as problematic by those who have yet to consciously move away from their own biases.

Perhaps one of the reasons why flexing this advocacy muscle continues to be such a deep-rooted issue for women in particular is that it intersects so closely with the likability factor. This arbitrary way of judging women based on subjective factors that can influence their ability to be "liked" happens on so many conscious and subconscious levels. Women tend to go out of their way to be team players, exuding waves of warmth so as not to be punished for being too assertive, too direct, or too ambitious. We worry about being labeled "bossy," "bitchy," or "selfish," while men are lauded as being "competent" or "confident" when using the same type of communication. (Throw these gender stereotypes on top of being a woman of color, and it's a double whammy.)

Take, for example, the following informal experiment conducted by Columbia Business School professor Frank Flynn. He split up his class into two groups and presented the first group with a case study from Harvard Business School on Heidi Roizen, a successful businesswoman and entrepreneur in Silicon Valley. It detailed Roizen's career path and the challenges she faced. The second group was presented with the same case study of Heidi's career experience, but with one amendment: Heidi's name was changed to Howard. Both groups were asked to rate the person they had read about. The difference in the answers was that, although Heidi seemed just as competent as Howard to the students, the majority of them judged her negatively; she didn't seem likable to them, and she wasn't someone they'd want to work with or even hire. The more assertive they thought Heidi was, the more harshly they judged her. This was not the case for those who rated Howard, whom the students deemed more likable.

This experiment is emblematic of the problem women in the professional world at large face. When women become more assertive—whether it be with the language we use, our approach to problem-solving, or our leadership style—we tend to be penalized. Why? Because being assertive contradicts the gendered stereotypes about women that have long held us back: that we're always agreeable, that we're people-oriented, that we take care of everyone first. There's a classic saying in Spanish, "Calladita te ves más bonita," meaning women look better if we remain quiet. It's a mentality that has been perpetuated and accepted for generations, and it's always in the background as girls and women process information about what is expected of us versus how we show up in real life.

According to research by social and organizational psychologist Madeline E. Heilman, who studies gender stereotypes and workplace bias, our ideas about what male and female roles "should" be can perpetuate gender bias by leading us to assume women are not fit to be successful in positions and roles that are gender-typed as male. Likewise, if the stereotypes about women say that we're congenial, communal team players who use accommodating language, and these qualities are considered inherent to women, we may experience disapproval and social penalties when we violate these stereotypes (or when others simply perceive that we have violated them).

As I started my career, I was less interested in being liked and more worried about being taken seriously and respected. I had a chip on my shoulder about making change in my own path to create opportunity, and I was proud of it. So I wasn't too concerned about bringing forth my intensity, which manifested itself in my young twentysomething passion and polite self-assuredness. But that didn't always mean people were on board with it.

My mom found my respectful-yet-direct manner of expressing

myself straight-up abrasive. She'd often advise me to be less harsh in tone. Culturally speaking, Latinos are used to infusing the long-winded romanticism of the Spanish language into all aspects of life; we value interactions and people who opt for social amicability. Any International Business 101 class will teach you that when doing business in Latin America, establishing rapport, building relationships, getting people to like you, and exuding friendship-like qualities will allow you to win over the boss and close the deal. The process of relationship-building can be just as important as the end goal, which can make us at times somewhat less direct than, say, people from the United States.

Being too direct as a woman can be off-putting, and as a woman of color? Even worse! I like to cut through all the fluff and get to the point, which my grandma said just showed how "gringa" I had become. Honestly, this didn't faze me much, because I fully embraced being assertive. But once, my own intensity and cut-to-the-chase way of talking, unbeknownst to me, almost cost me a job opportunity.

I sat in a conference room in front of three high-level company executives, ready for a job interview. I was a nervous wreck, but as a result of working for years in front of strangers in their homes as a Mary Kay consultant, I kept faithfully to my chin-up, smiling, shoulders-back, open stance. One of the executives took the lead in the conversation, which I thought was going pretty well. I felt confident that my message was coming across effectively. And a few weeks later, I got the job and never looked back.

Then, a few years ago, I had a chance to meet with one of the three executives who had interviewed me that day. As we spoke over coffee about the progression of our careers, our conversation steered to that first interview. It turns out that after our meeting, one of the interviewers (who no longer works at that company) expressed to the other two that she was worried I might be "difficult" to work with, especially taking into account that this job would require me to rotate around different parts of the company and have a lot of external interface with different employees and work cultures. Her hesitancy came down to one question: whether or not I would get along with others and be "liked."

Huh. I was not expecting that.

Sure, in interviews and any other high-stakes situations, I aim to make sure that whoever I'm speaking to knows how serious I am about the role and how I'd approach my work, and I suppose it can come across as direct. I'm clear about the value I offer. But *unlikable*? I was in no way curt, impolite, or rude. Thankfully, the other two interviewers likely realized that my intensity would translate into hard work and efficiency. It probably helped that one of them also had immigrant family ties and understood that the passion with which I spoke about my story indicated qualities that would *aid* my work life, not detract from it. I was lucky that there were three interviewers and not one.

Learning about this—even though it was years later and I was well on my way up the career ladder—brought to light how many unfair standards women, especially minority women, are held to, as well as the self-monitoring we're supposed to do. Would this interviewer have said the same of a young white man expressing with intensity how his background shaped his work ethic? I'd guess that, on the contrary, it would be a testament to his self-assurance and competence, which we expect from men more consistently than from women. Did the fact that I was Latina and speaking with passion make me come off as hysterical or maybe just "too much"? There's no way of knowing, but I must admit it was like a tiny, sharp gut punch to my confidence. It goes to show how much is at stake for women of color and minorities and all that we have to deal with as we contend with the ever-present bias and blind spots that still exist in the workplace.

But the reality is that there's too much at stake for us to succumb to those voices that make us doubt whether it's okay to say what we mean and mean what we say concisely and directly. Why are we carrying the weight of someone else's inability to see women in powerful, strong, assertive roles? That's on them! There's an inherent need to self-correct, yet when we play into the very stereotypes people expect of us, we are only strengthening the very gender bias that is holding us back. What we really need to do is embrace our voice and say, *I'm not interested in your cognitive dissonance!* The same could be said about racial bias or any form of assumptions or misguided beliefs about a given community or group. It's not our responsibility to correct them, but we can prove them wrong through our own actions and ability to push through by clearly vocalizing and showing our own value.

We've seen how the cumulatively detrimental results of gender and racial bias aggravate the gender pay gap, lower our wages, and perpetuate a lack of promotions, career development, and access to opportunities to get ourselves in the door. All of this makes us feel like, somehow, we're the ones doing something wrong. We start treading lightly for fear of what reactions standing our ground could provoke in others. We allow *their* shortcomings to affect our sense of self and question our own abilities. We become afraid of our own power!

Speaking up, advocating for yourself—at the end of the day, this isn't just for us at an individual level. Not allowing ourselves to express who we are, what we bring to the table, and what we want to achieve carries far more weight than our individual needs. Our diverse voices and perspectives will also help give rise to other voices. Everything we do helps build upon that foundation. We have too much to lose when we don't speak up; there's so much at stake when we don't fully show up. And I mean this in every way possible. Our advocating power is our greatest tool. Used effectively, it can help break generational poverty when we negotiate our worth. It can amplify our stories, our perspectives, our lived experiences. It can help others feel seen and valued in the process.

Advocating effectively in the workplace helps us move forward and work toward putting more women from Black, Asian American, Latina, Native American, and other minority communities at the top of leadership. But we have to do it collectively, at every step, at every opportunity we get. We have to continue to push aside the fear, nervousness, hesitancy, self-judgment, and internal chatter that get in our way, because our success as women isn't just our own; it affects the success of our families, our communities, our economy, and the path we leave for young women after us.

Owning your voice and narrative means owning your power. The more we tap into that power, the more we make room for each and every one of our widely different, inspiring, and enriching stories. When we bring up other women with us—whether it's speaking well of them in front of others when they're not in the room, mentoring them, or sponsoring an opportunity they otherwise wouldn't have had—we are helping to level the playing field and amplify our own voices by elevating our sisterhood in the workplace.

It's time to use your voice to contribute to the change you want to see for yourself and others. Every time you find confidence in advocating for yourself, you influence the opportunities and examples you set for those that come after you.

10

Go for More!

Day after day, we dedicate eight, nine, ten, or more hours to creating, producing, and doing work for our employer. We show up and devote our time, effort, skills, networks, and know-how to the job. We may even put our personal lives on hold to develop our careers and move up this promised ladder of success. Yet in my years of writing and reporting on women at work, I've continuously found one disappointing truth: the more educated women are, particularly those from minority communities, the more they pay a price in evolving and getting paid what they're worth.

According to a study on Latina women in the United States published by NBCUniversal Telemundo Enterprises and Comcast NBCUniversal, "Latinas who have obtained an associate's degree or higher on average earn a third of what non-Hispanic white males with similar educational profiles earn." In terms of equal pay, Latinas lag farther behind white men than any other demographic of women. In 2021, Latinas earned a meager 57 cents for every dollar a white man earned, according to the US Department of Labor. (For Black women it's 64 cents, and for white women it's 79 cents.) It makes zero sense.

I spend time in conversation with many women of color who live out these statistics in Acceso, my mentorship community—hardworking, roll-up-your-sleeves type women with degrees—and I've come to learn that aside from the failure of institutions to create more opportunities for advancement (and pay transparency—so overdue!), our negotiating muscle plays a crucial role too. We should expect to be paid fairly, accurately, and, at the very least, at market rate. But we know that, in reality, it doesn't always play out that way for women of color, who often face a real backlash when asking for more in the workplace. Yet there is a dire need for us to become our own best advocates when demanding the pay, roles, and access that we deserve and need in order to climb the ladder toward the type of success we seek.

A key component is to negotiate strategically. As important as it for our career success, it's not something we often grew up hearing about or discussing with our own families. I certainly didn't. So we need to flex that muscle and get smart about how we do it. Whether you are negotiating your salary or your next promotion, it's as much about what you ask for as how you ask.

Asking for more at work is never easy. We know this. It's uncomfortable, awkward, and confusing. We can't control a lot of outside entities, and we also can't wait to get better or create change. It's time for us to step up our advocating and negotiating game—something that we do have control over. Being more vocal about your own advancement is crucial. Make sure you're clearly articulating your worth to others and that your salary and job responsibilities adequately reflect that.

The first step is to get into the right mindset. There's no room for a million different scattered thoughts in the negotiating room. Asking for more can lead to a wave of insecurities and false self-talk that you need to get in check before you enter any conversation with someone about what you want. *Do they remember that time I messed up? Am I really ready for this? What if they say no?* All of this self-chatter needs to be dealt with beforehand. Because when you go for it, you want to be completely clear. An avalanche of destructive thoughts will only distract you from why you're walking into that room in the first place.

Before you go in there, get those thoughts out of your system and focus on taking away their power over you. Write them down, make them visible. Read them, and then ask yourself, *What does any of this have to do with asking this company for fair compensation in exchange for my work?* I bet the answer will be: *Nothing.* Because that's all this is: a simple input and output scenario. Labor for wages. It's not personal. At the end of the day, none of these thoughts are going to get you what you want, so toss them in the trash and keep your eye on the ball.

I love this piece of advice shared with me by Dia Simms, former president of Combs Enterprises and current CEO at Lobos 1707 tequila, about the mindset she employs around negotiations, both in her early career and in the multimillion-dollar partnerships she's negotiated at the companies she's worked for: "I decide what outcome I am after and ground the negotiation in my objective. It is better to take leadership and set the negotiation boundaries up front versus waiting for someone to tell you your worth. Practice this in a mirror and with a trusted friend."

So let's be clear: What exactly are you asking for? More money, more flexibility, more leadership opportunities? Whatever it may be, it's crucial you narrow it down and get really specific to back up your ask with the right argument. This way you can focus on concrete evidence for each ask instead of going in there and word-vomiting a list of needs and wants that will sound scattered.

My first promotion came about two years into my first job as a production coordinator for *Morning Joe*. I'd get to the studio set at four a.m., then work late into the evenings and on weekends. During that time, I racked up a lot of overtime. It was a role that gave me the leverage to be able to point to a lot of different examples of the value I brought to my job, but it could have easily been a role in which I missed my chance to advance because I already felt fulfilled, useful, and needed. I was comfortable in this role, I was good at it, and I could have easily stayed there longer.

About a year and a half in, I was tapped for a promotion in the booking department as a junior booker. I was confident I had what it took to get to the next step and that whatever new skills I needed for booking I could learn quickly, but did I know how to translate that into the money I deserved? I wasn't sure. I was just thankful to get a chance to be there and eternally grateful to be considered for this new role. As we've discussed before, I feared that if I asked for more, I'd be seen as ungrateful and replaceable.

So when they offered me a higher-ranking role with a lower salary than I had been making for the first year and a half to two years, I was conflicted. Should I take the higher role and forgo the income I had been making?

What I realized is that if I did that, it wouldn't just affect my earning potential for the next few years; it would snowball, jeopardizing my salary negotiations for years to come. Studies show that women start out earning at a lower rate than their male counterparts and rarely catch up. We all have a duty to advocate for ourselves and ask for more, not just individually but as a collective, because what we each achieve today helps chip away at the overall wage gap in a cumulative way.

So I got specific and came back with a number that at least put me in line with the salary I had been paid, including overtime, for the two years prior. My responsibilities would only be getting more complex and demanding. I knew I needed the money to match it. Yet the idea of asking someone else to agree to a number that translated into my worth felt so uncomfortable. As if it were a personal reflection of who I was as a person. Even when I received the money for coauthoring my first book, there was something about it that also made me uneasy—like I wasn't supposed to be making that much more on top of my salary. As if the added $50,000 I made from the book meant I shouldn't ask for more at my current job. I didn't realize how backward that thinking was, especially since they are two different roles completely independent of each other. But the feelings were still there, and they translated into unnecessary mental clutter.

In order to jump this negotiating hurdle, I had to get to the core emotions around my inability to talk about money. Subconsciously, I felt guilty. I was asking for a figure that, in my household, even with my parents working two or three jobs at a time, was unimaginably high. But in reality, one thing had nothing to do with the other. What's more, the book advance I received was for a job I was doing on the weekends and in my own free time, which had nothing to do with the countless hours of work I put in at my day job.

It's that internal debate of our value that can be a huge issue for us. Men are better at this; they don't negotiate against themselves with their feelings as often as we do.

When Leticia, a member of Acceso, was getting ready to start negotiations for her first brand partnership, she felt completely intimidated and didn't know where to begin. She had spent years working on her own consulting business, creating and developing an exclusive learning curriculum as part of the courses she taught. This meant years of developing original content, of sacrificing family time, of putting in extra hours without knowing how or if it would all pay off. Initially, she had been consulting for individuals and small businesses, until she got this opportunity to partner with a big-name brand. It was a chance to take her business to the next level, but it was uncharted territory. She didn't know what rates to offer or how to go about asking for what her services were worth, and she wondered if she'd be taken seriously when it came down to negotiating terms of the partnership. Similar to employees with roles that don't have industry-standard pay bands, it's not like she could go on Glassdoor.com and see what other entrepreneurs were charging for their partnership deals. What's more, partnership deals vary by the size of the business you're partnering with—bigger companies have bigger budgets.

Leticia knew all of this, and she knew she had to go for it and ask for more, but doubts riddled her mind: *What if they change their mind and don't want to work with me anymore?* Even though the higher rates she wanted to negotiate as part of the terms of her contract were more than she was used to, she knew they were in line with the big bucks this company was used to shelling out. Yet she felt that asking for more could put her deal in jeopardy.

It was incumbent on Leticia to mentally prepare herself and talk herself up when she was in front of them. She needed to invoke all the hard work she had put forth and realize that she'd be selling herself short if she allowed herself to be swayed by that fear that told her it was too risky to ask for the amount she was gunning for.

So I advised her to make a list, in detail, of all the sacrifices—big and small—she had gone through to develop her business: the recitals she had to miss, the times the bills almost didn't get paid, the late nights and sleep-deprived days when she threw herself into the mission of growing and creating her exclusive curriculum. Then I asked her to make a list of the reasons why she had poured so much of herself into this business: the communities that were affected by the content of her message, financial security for her family, growing a team of her own one day. This was not material I wanted her to bring to the negotiating table—this was exclusively for her. Instead of leaning in with fear, she could use the emotions behind these lists to make a difference in how she showed up to negotiate that day. It helped her reframe the component of risk she felt going in and asking for more; it was clear to her now she had too much to risk *by not* asking for what she deemed appropriate compensation in the partnership deal. What's more, it helped her amplify the worth she ascribed to her own work and recognized that it was important for her to work with a company that acknowledged that worth themselves; and that meant paying her, her worth. Calm, confident, and assertive, she now had a clear understanding of how to combat those feelings of insecurity, and nothing was going to stop her.

She was emboldened by her own work, by reminding herself of the sacrifice, the time, the effort, and all the other paid and unpaid work that she went through to uphold her skill set and this original content she had created. This confidence came from a deep place of knowing she had worked harder than anyone to create something unique and her own. She wasn't going to let any emotions of doubt or fear stand in the way of asking for what she rightfully deserved. This list wasn't what she was using to make her case on the numbers she wanted. It was for her to understand why she needed to get out of her own head and get into a winning and assertive mindset: She had totally earned it.

On the more practical side, to inform how much money she was going to ask for, she did her research on the numbers side of things, speaking to other consultants who had made the jump to work with big brand names and studying the market for comparable rates. Even if the numbers are not as transparent and visible as you'd like (how you need them to be, frankly), you have to get used to talking about them and asking others about them. Start with people in your circle, and don't be afraid to be honest: "I am doing research on the market rate for my role, and if you're comfortable, I'd love to know if you have any insight or would be willing to share a ballpark salary range with me to help me navigate my own negotiations." And if it's someone you're comfortable with, ask: "Who would you recommend I speak to who is or has been in a similar role and might be comfortable sharing this type of information?"

Women of color are so often in the dark about the *real numbers*. The numbers white men make, and often white women too. Let's get over our fear and hesitancy of talking about money and just remember this when we start to feel hesitant about broaching this subject. We have too much to lose.

When you go to the negotiating table, remember to go in there assertively and keep your *why* in mind for confidence. Period. We have to acknowledge the facets of the labor we do and not be ashamed of talking about money—because we can't talk about our value if we can't talk about the money that comes with it. A great tip I learned early on: It's not personal; it's business.

Now that we've gotten the money talk out of the way, it's time to focus on your delivery. How many times have you been in the negotiating room and tried to fill the room up with words at the smallest hint of silence? How many times have you started a conversation about your salary or a potential promotion with "I'm sorry, I know this might be a bad time, but..." or "I may be wrong here, but..."? And how many times have you just word-vomited so much that you actually talked someone out of giving you what you want? Many of us have been in a place where we've decided to ask for a promotion or a raise, we've named the price, stated why and then... silence. And suddenly we follow with something impulsive to fill up the awkward silence in the room, like, "But I totally understand if not!" or "I can be flexible if that doesn't sound right," or "Of course, I can make whatever works for you work."

These types of qualifiers undermine us before we even get a

chance to state our positions or opinions. We're more likely than men to look for ways to soften our language for fear of sounding too harsh. That natural inclination to make everyone else in the room feel comfortable with our presence, which we've discussed earlier in the book, becomes a huge liability in the negotiating room for women of color and other marginalized groups, who are by and large disproportionally burdened in the workplace by uncompensated work. To negotiate like a boss, practice clear and direct language to articulate your points, and, even if you feel like you're jumping out of your skin, embrace the power of the pause or silence.

In her book *Ask for More*, Alexandra Carter, a well-regarded negotiating expert and Columbia law professor, describes the power of sitting in silence after making your ask at work as "landing the plane." When I spoke to her about this need to fill the room with words, she gave me the example of a Black woman she once coached—let's call her Alice—who, after earning her MBA, was being recruited by a big-name company for an executive role. In the interview, the company higher-ups kept raving about how committed they were to diversity, equity, and inclusion. Alice ended up getting the job. What they didn't tell her was that, on top of her day-to-day duties, she would also be sent to countless recruiting events and panels, and would be asked to mentor other Black women in the company. Her schedule quickly became overburdened with tasks that frankly weren't giving her the skills she needed to build in order to advance and get promoted.

Alex advised her to go in and renegotiate the terms of her workload. Alice called a meeting with her business unit and DEI (Diversity, Equity, and Inclusion). She pointed out clearly and without beating around the bush that, although asking her to be included and front-facing for DEI efforts was necessary work the company should be doing, it was also taking up tremendous time and effort that kept her from work that would help her advance. She asked for them to show equal enthusiasm in creating opportunities for her advancement as they did in putting her in front of their DEI initiative. Then, she landed the plane—she let them sit in silence for a moment and reflect on the import of her words.

The people she was negotiating with quickly got the point. They agreed and worked to rectify the problem by giving her access to higher-caliber client work. They also assigned her mentors to make sure there was follow-through on the actions the company had agreed to take.

Alice's approach worked for several reasons. First, the stakes were clear. She laid out the data regarding the work she had been given and how exactly it was holding her back from other projects.

Second, she proposed a solution-driven ask that was in her interest *and* theirs, since they both wanted to foster a workplace where she could succeed and thrive. She articulated that clearly, without leaving any details up for interpretation. She knew they needed her, and in return she needed them to practice what they preached. During our conversation, Dia Simms also echoed great advice: "The best negotiators know how to clearly paint the opportunity for both sides. People are motivated by outcomes where they benefit. Employ empathy in your negotiation, and be sure to clearly identify what's in it for the other side. In a career setting, it typically costs a company six to nine months of an employee's salary to replace him/her. Retention is much cheaper than recruitment. It is in the company's best interest to keep great employees, exceedingly so in today's climate." Ask yourself this question: *What am I uniquely bringing to this negotiation that is not easy to replace?*

Third, Alice expressed her message effectively. No filler words. No trying to make them feel comfortable first. She made her point with rock-solid certainty, because she knew the value she brought to the table. And then she paused. Silence. That's when she landed the plane.

Research presented in the article "Silence Is Golden" in the *Journal of Applied Psychology* shows that after three seconds of silence, you have a better chance of getting higher value out of your negotiation or ask. By letting silence fill the room after making an ask, you give the other person the chance and space to think about what you've just articulated, and they become more likely to agree with what you've proposed. Never underestimate the power of the pause, especially if you usually feel the need to immediately accommodate and appease others.

Power in silence is useful even outside the moment of negotiation itself. It also comes in handy when you want to make sure you're getting a good deal. In other words, if you're the one being presented an offer, and you're unsure if it's the most beneficial scenario or offers the best terms, take a beat. You don't need to give them an answer immediately. As Alex puts it, "Other people's urgency is not *your* urgency." Don't rush to accommodate, because you might make a decision that doesn't serve your best interests. Take your time responding. "Thank you, I'm going to take a few days to consider the option/offer." You've now changed the power dynamic.

Okay, so, what if you check off all these negotiating boxes, confidently walk into that room, and slay your presentation, but you're still met by a no?

Don't let that one word bring you tumbling down. Don't let it destroy your confidence and all your hard work. That no is not personal. That no is not saying that you are less than or that you don't belong. That no is business. So instead of allowing it to discourage you, instead of running away from that answer and hiding in your cubicle, figure out exactly *why* you got a no. Is it because of company financials? Skills they've pointed out you need to work on? Something else? Make note of these answers, then ask them questions that will help set you up with specific metrics that would lead that no into yes territory.

Think of the questions you're going to ask to follow up. You have to focus negotiating talks on pure objectives. If it's because of company financials, ask for a timeline on when you can talk again: "When can I set time on your calendar to revisit this conversation?" If it's gaps in your experience, ask how they're measuring your success: "What are your concerns going forward, and what specific metrics are you looking for?" Then lay out a plan of action to fill those gaps so that you can actively prepare for that next step. No more beating around the bush and leaving the meeting confused or unsure about the next step. This way there's no guessing if you and the decision maker are on the same page. There's a lot at stake for you, so make sure to know exactly what was missing between that no and yes, and why.

Asking questions also gets the person you're working with invested in your development, and it gives you a chance to strengthen your data points and arguments for when you return to the negotiating table. That no doesn't mean you can never again advocate for yourself in this way. It just means you need to wait for the right time, and in the meantime, you can prep yourself or develop further, so that you can walk into that room in three, six, eight months, and ask again.

We are now working on a playing field that is far more advantageous to women than it was years ago. Women understand more than ever that we have to get comfortable asking for pay that is in line with our value. And employers are getting used to hearing it.

This is about principles beyond our individual worth—although our individual worth is already incredibly important. It is about breaking generational barriers. It's about building generational wealth for ourselves, our families, and our communities. This is where our ability to talk about money, advocate for ourselves fiercely, and negotiate strategically has the power to move those pitiful numbers in the wage gap once and for all. Let's ask for the damn money—we need it, and we deserve it. Let's all be part of that change.

11

Your Career Needs a Manager

Once you decide to fully show up as yourself, that's when you really start to pragmatically set a different tone for yourself and your career. Let's say you're now in command of your messaging, and you're noticing a shift in the way others are responding to you. Not only are you speaking up for yourself to get what you want, but you're also starting to show up with a new energy. You know your unique worth and understand that your knowledge and experience is v-a-l-u-a-b-l-e. You're on your way to becoming your very own trailblazer. This new confidence is helping set the tone that you want in your career going forward, and actively contributing to the growth that you're seeking. Now that your stock value is up, it's important to know how to best leverage it to manage your career effectively.

Keep coming back to the principles in this book whenever doubt tries to creep into your growth. Stay attuned to your strength. Don't doubt yourself. The truth is, the sky is the limit from where you are now. You may be an assistant, manager, executive, or entrepreneur, but no matter what your role is, you have the power to set the tone of your career and forge ahead. How do you tap into that trailblazer mentality? Start by developing your leadership style.

Leadership isn't just about leading an organization or a group of people. It's about setting the tone in our careers, managing them, and, most importantly, owning our professional narrative and showing others how to treat us. You don't have to wait until you land a leadership role to act like a leader. When we start to consciously think of ourselves as innovators, trendsetters, and leaders, we're inviting others to see us in that light too. It's about gaining leverage in our organizations so we can effectively do our jobs and create change, if that's what we want. Leadership also means taking up space.

Taking up space—that's something you've probably heard on repeat lately. It's become a favorite go-to catchphrase for any advice related to professional growth. For me, that phrase means being able to step into the workplace with command and power in a way that gathers your best strengths and exhibits the best of your leadership style, giving you the ability to influence others and have a prime seat at the table. When you take up space, you say what you mean and mean what you say; you express your ideas clearly and articulately. Whatever self-limiting beliefs you might have don't get in the way of your professional messaging. You feel worthy of the space that you're taking up, and, more important, you understand more than anyone else how valuable you are to that space, especially because of the added value that you, as a minority or person of color, contribute to your workplace.

In 2019, I was invited to take the stage at the Forbes Under 30 Summit in Detroit, Michigan, as part of a panel on financial health, due in part to my writing and reporting for NBC's Know Your Value about financial literacy and personal finance from the perspective of communities of color, specifically of minority women.

At this point in my career, I hadn't been on many public stages, and certainly none that faced hundreds of audience members like that day. Minutes before going on, I had another one of those *How the hell did I get here?* moments as the setting sunk in. The other panelists that I'd be joining actually had full-time jobs related to financial literacy. One was a female executive, and the other was an author of a *New York Times* best-selling book on financial health. Both were thought leaders in this space.

But I reminded myself that, although I had not dedicated my entire career to this space, I had spent a good amount of time on topics that are often overlooked and that would be an important piece of the conversation we'd be having onstage: the issues unique to communities of color that hold us back when it comes to financial empowerment, and the frustration of seeing blanket financial advice that often doesn't consider the lived experiences and challenges of minorities. And I knew that my stories and reporting had struck a chord with readers, so I held my own. My reporting contextualized the nuances surrounding that conversation while keeping in mind the extra hurdles women of color face that I felt were often left out of the conversation, such as the caretaking aspects of our communities, the need to overcome guilt to create generational wealth, the role of family in decision-making, and so on.

The next day, I was scheduled to co-moderate a debate among Republican presidential hopefuls, so instead of leaving right after my panel, I went back to my room to prep. That night, I received an email that had "Serena Williams" in the subject line. Intrigued, I opened it, assuming it was a pitch for *Morning Joe*. It was actually from one of Serena Williams's public relations professionals, who mentioned she'd caught my panel earlier that day and had been impressed. Serena was the keynote speaker for the entire Forbes conference and had partnered with a well-known company to talk about financial abuse in communities of color. She was going to be taking the stage the next day. "We are only giving one interview with her and we're wondering if you'd be interested," said the message.

Excuse me?

Dumbfounded, I immediately started churning through ideas on how to make this work. Technically I was a booking producer, not a correspondent for my network, so how would I get the interview on *Morning Joe* without a camera crew? High on adrenaline, I started to break down what I needed to do next.

I was granted this interview because of my reporting style and unique perspective, I thought to myself, overcome with nerves. If I really wanted to be seen as a journalist who could be on air as well as behind the camera, I needed to show hard evidence that I could do just that. I had already done red carpets and shorter digital interviews for NBC's Know Your Value platform, but nothing for broadcast. Since this was outside of my job description, I needed to show that I could do it, that I could pull off the logistics, and that even though I didn't have a lot of practice, I could pull off the interview with the legend and queen Serena

Williams! There was no hand-holding to be had—the time had come to show my boss what I could do, even though I had less experience than everyone else. I would have to figure out quickly how to be a reporter.

Okay, I thought. The whole summit was being recorded, and I had seen backstage videographers, so I emailed the event organizers, thinking, *Surely, there has to be some crew capability here.* The request traveled up to the chief content officer, and sure enough, they could make it work—it was also a clear win for them to host a televised interview. After securing my crew, I emailed my boss. "I have a crew in place. I'm ready to produce and do the interview, and I can offer an extended version to be featured online for our Know Your Value platform. I just need your green light."

I set it up so that it was a win-win for everyone. Serena's people were happy because their initiative was going to be on national news, it was a high-quality production, and it would be featured on a website very much in line with their mission.

I replaced *Am I really qualified to do this?* with *How do I turn this seemingly impossible task into a reality?* It was my time to take action and take up space. It meant seeing myself beyond the expectations around my day job as a booking producer, and figuring out how to make each step happen, from the production to getting it on the air, and negotiating potential benefits for everyone involved.

I was proud that I got the yes from my boss, who was ultimately putting himself on the line by letting me transform into an instant reporter without much experience—and doing it with a major figure like Serena Williams. He could have easily given me a pat on the back for getting us the interview and suggested that I ask someone else to do it in my place. But I had gone to him confidently ready to work around the nuances and sensitivities of the whole undertaking. The key was understanding that when your colleagues and higher-ups are running a mile a minute with their own to-do lists, the more you can serve them your intended execution and results on a platter, the more likely it is you'll be given a shot.

If you're ever up for an opportunity to show your ability to lead, go for it. Find ways to show hard evidence that they should trust you to follow through and get the job done. It can feel like a scary, unprecedented risk that might cause people to judge you or say, "Who does she think she is?" But actually it's an opportunity for you to play bigger. That's how leaders think. That will be the difference between you and everyone else. Stepping up to the plate, psyching yourself up, and then following through with deliverables.

For me it went back to my *why*, which we discussed earlier. My writing on women of color and financial health was not something that was part of my job—or that I was even being paid for at the time—but it was the type of storytelling that connected to what I felt was the purpose of my career: helping empower women. This opportunity came about because I had released any fear of authentically bringing my community into the fold of my work, even when it meant going against the grain or bringing up information that traditionally might be talked about less. After that experience with Serena Williams, I proved to others—and more importantly to myself—that I could strategically create new value in my role.

Sometimes, taking initiative without waiting for someone else to direct you has more cumulative power than you think. Sometimes the best opportunities require drawing outside the lines and doing things unconventionally, if it's not going to really jeopardize your job safety. Sometimes all of these seeming setbacks ultimately lead to something bigger. Is there an initiative you could bring up and lead? An analysis you can create to show new data or a new partnership you can cultivate and bring into the company's fold? Whatever it may be, go for it.

While writing my first book, I met a woman who embodies leadership in ways that redefine what traditional leadership looks like. Anjali Sud, who became the youngest CEO at Vimeo at age thirty-three, is someone I think defines what it means to be an authentic trailblazer. As a CEO in her thirties, she doesn't try to be something she's not. "I do not try to dress older," she told me. "I do not try and communicate in a way that the traditional stereotype of a CEO might. I try and be myself. I try to normalize my experience with my team, by being open about things like my pregnancy, or that time I burst into tears at a meeting. I find my energy and passion to be core to how I lead." That conversation stuck with me. Even as a CEO, she figured out how to communicate and operate with ease, in a way that feels more in tune and authentic to her than what any leadership playbook would recommend, and that, in turn, affects and strengthens her style.

But wait, what does showing up as our authentic self in the workplace really mean for those of us who may not be CEO? Good leadership does require a certain etiquette. Authenticity is not a hall pass for completely loose behavior. In any corporate or workplace environment there are nuances, workflows, and overall institutional bureaucracy that need to be considered and consulted. But there are still ways to bring your true self into those spaces and thrive.

At my core, and with the people I consider my close circle, I am, at times, admittedly dramatic. I can't bring all of that to work. I live for a good chisme and tend to feel my emotions deeply. Hey, if there's no need for a filter, why hide what feels natural? I'm also partial to sarcasm and my true OGs get my dry sense of humor. As an introvert, I get easily drained by small talk, and I can be very sensitive, so I cry often. Do I want or need to bring *all* of that to the workplace? Nope!

Bring your best and most unique qualities to work so that you are respected, heard, and able to progress in your career. You can be and act authentically within the boundaries of what your job requires of you. There's a middle point—that separation between work and our personal self that won't distract your messaging but will make you distinct and amplify your value to yourself and others.

I may write or speak about my personal experiences in my work, and I've become used to writing with vulnerability and transparency about parts of me that I used to hide. It hasn't always been easy—yet it has helped me home in on my own voice. It's scary and often uncomfortable, but it actually resonates with others, and that's why I do it. Still, it's important for me to draw a line and know what is appropriate and not with my day job. In this day and age, I think we can get carried away with the word "authentic." For our own emotional safety, we can choose what we want to show and what we don't in a professional setting, and that doesn't mean we're not being true to ourselves. Sometimes work is just work.

The truth is that not everyone will receive your authenticity as a leader the same way, and that's beyond your control. Companies and leaders have their own work to do—their own conscious and unconscious biases to overcome—to create more room for women of color to feel safe bringing their unique qualities to work. Calling on us for (largely unpaid) diversity and inclusion efforts or recruitment opportunities is not enough.

We are speaking up about important issues, and for the first time, accountability is taking center stage in certain industries. We are at a precipice, a point in history where, if leaders and companies are unwilling or unable to keep up, or bank on making empty promises, they will be left behind, and they will suffer the consequences.

At the same time, there's work we can do to help make these companies aware of what is no longer working and what needs to change. I've heard plenty of times from women of color that they're hired to jobs that preach about inclusivity and changes, but when they have that seat at the table they're told in no uncertain terms that there's no room for new ideas or ways of thinking. That's why leadership, controlling our messaging, and taking up space on our own terms all play a key role in how we can help impact and empower our communities. For you that may mean deciding on going out on your own or even reconsidering your place of work to find one that really values you doing the work you were hired for.

Julissa Prado, the creator of hair-product company Rizos Curls, is a trailblazer who, before starting her own brand, held corporate leadership positions at Nestlé. This experience gave her knowledge on the consumer-goods ecosystem, which provided her with essential information when it came time for her to know the worth of her own business. She had initially planned to balance her corporate job and Rizos Curls, and that worked out for the first four years during the product-development stage, but once she launched, she received so many orders that she realized if she wanted to really get this off the ground, it would take her undivided attention just to keep up with the demand alone. So she quit Nestlé. What had started out as her side project soon became her full-time job.

Lack of funding is a pervasive problem for entrepreneurs of color, but Julissa got around it by being 100 percent self-funded. She achieved this by bringing her family into the fold to work on everything from the design and packaging to the marketing of her products. Julissa intrinsically knew the value of her business and the product she offered; it was personal to her. So she started small and rejected the idea that she had to be backed by big funding to get her products sold in a major retailer. Instead, she followed her own playbook and went on to achieve what many had told her was impossible: becoming the first Latina-owned curly haircare brand to launch at Target, Ulta Beauty, and Sally Beauty Mexico.

Her products at Target sold out in two days. Then, when she launched at Ulta Beauty, she only had $1,000 for marketing and advertising. She got around the low budget by tapping into the power of social media, where she focused all of her marketing on TikTok. She had an outside-the-box idea, but she stuck to her guns and followed through with it confidently. She decided to show up at the Ulta Beauty store event in Los Angeles on a horse, with a lovebird parrot perched on her shoulder, followed by a parade of her friends and family and a trail of mariachis, low riders, and a paleta cart, all of which she rented with the small budget. If you follow Julissa, you know this is a very on-brand moment. It was all captured on TikTok, and the #RizosCurlsAt-Ulta hashtag went viral, receiving more than 8 million views on TikTok alone. The result? Her products sold out within a matter of days on Ulta Beauty's website.

"My greatest strength is my community," Julissa told me, "and I've been able to build my business from the ground up while being self-funded by staying true to my community and my mission."

Julissa's *why* has made her a trailblazer in her field, and it has remained the motivation on every step of her journey and within every challenge. Her mission helps her bring her big ideas to bear, and will hopefully ultimately open doors for others and help drive inclusivity.

"I learned early on that just because something hasn't happened before doesn't mean that it's not possible," she said to me. "There's always more than one right way to do things." This might as well be my life motto.

There's too much to lose when we don't bring our creativity and unique cultural duality to the table. We can't wait for companies or our bosses or teams to do it for us!

There are hundreds of companies, big and small, that are being called out on their bias and are experiencing internal upheavals on a daily basis—even if they're not happening in the public eye—in large part because employees of color are fed up, and they're using their voices to speak out and push back. Inequities aren't built to last. The more we try to push back and assert ourselves, the bigger the part we play in breaking down those inequities. Pushing back effectively is a crucial rule of leadership. When you've earned your way to more but fear pushing back, and instead succeed by accommodating everyone else, you are giving away power.

Laura, a mentee in Acceso Community, worked in the manufacturing industry at the same job for a decade. Five and a half years in, she made the decision to come out as gay to her employer and colleagues. She remembers it to the day because it took her four years to feel comfortable enough in her job to decide to do it, and then another one and a half years to plan out exactly how to do it.

In the years after that, she used her role as one of the first openly gay employees as an opportunity to pave the way for inclusivity at her organization. She knew it took courage and a sense of acceptance to make the plunge, so she helped form the first LGBTQ resource group so others wouldn't feel so alone. One of the first projects she created during the first year of the resource group was a company initiative spotlighting mid-level managers and executives who were LGBTQ allies. The key was to highlight these leaders as they spoke about why being an ally was important, in hopes it would act as a supportive nod to those who still might be in the shadows by letting them know it was safe to come out in the workplace.

To Laura's delight, the initiative was well received. She was one of the few women at the company (it was largely male-dominated) and one of only four openly LGBTQ employees at a global company with 30,000 employees in the United States alone, so the initial support was encouraging. Excited to keep it going, Laura had another idea on how to grow engagement for the group: give the LGBTQ members of the company a platform to share their story within the company, with profiles of executives speaking on allyship to be published internally, digital signage visible to visitors, mentions in company newsletters, and more.

But the answer was no.

The company blamed it on timing, claiming they had other initiatives in the queue they had to publish. Laura pushed back and voiced that it felt like discrimination. HR got involved. Still, nothing changed. They never published the feature in the company's newsletter highlighting the actual LGBTQ team members and were never able to come up with a solid reason as to why. Laura told me, "It became clear it was a check-the-box activity—they were willing to say they were allies but didn't want it to seem like we were shoving our stories down people's throats."

Turns out there were people at the company who weren't so supportive. One employee, in a company email sent to Laura, disclosed he was a pastor on the weekends and that he believed these initiatives by the LGBTQ resource group were wrong and sinful. Laura went to HR and was met with little help. "It's better not to answer back and let things like this resolve on their own," they said. It became clear that this company, as big of a conglomerate it was, and despite all the years Laura had dedicated to it, merely liked the *idea* of diversity and wanted little to do with true inclusion.

It's important to note here that some places, no matter how hard you try, will never change and meet you where you need them to in order to feel like you fully belong. This is an unfortunate reality. Efforts like those Laura spent time and energy on might have started to shift ideas and perspectives at that company incrementally, but at the end of the day, bigger changes require higher levels of leadership to step in. You don't have to carry a company's years of structural inequalities and generational viewpoints of prejudice on your shoulders. Laura was a leader and did her part. The closed-mindedness of others shouldn't have been her burden to bear. We deserve to make a living and follow a career in workplaces that accept the things about us that are important for our mental and emotional well-being. That's what lets us do our jobs effectively and not feel minimized. Don't settle for a workplace that wouldn't do otherwise.

Voicing her ideas to build inclusive visibility with a clear-cut plan was her way of pushing back, and although it didn't lead to structural change, it led to her planting the seeds of her own playbook and opening up a better job opportunity ahead, where she was valued and seen for who she is. Laura left that business and was recruited to a company where she was very upfront about being gay from the get-go, in the interview. She also created an LGBTQ resource group at this new company.

Yet her past experience impacted her ability to find her bearings as a leader in this place. "I felt like I needed permission for every topic I wanted to cover with the group and every communication I wanted to send," she told me. It wasn't until the executive sponsors asked her why she kept requesting permission at every turn and ultimately told her she should do what she thought was best, since she was the one leading the group, that she realized the dynamics here were different. Laura understood that her unfortunate experience in the past was just that: in the past. It didn't have to define how she should lead in this new job. She started to be more proactive and only went to her bosses for permission for the final green light instead of asking them what they thought at every turn. Laura was already in a director role and had more autonomy with her workflow, but for her to effectively be seen as a strong leader, she had to use the newfound leverage and power of her role and put the past behind her.

Even if you're not a CEO or director, you can still learn from Laura and Anjali. Now is your time to do what you can, to speak up and lead on everything from work-life balance to remote work options to leveraging your unique background. This is how you own your power as a woman of color or minority in the workplace. You simply lead, and don't look around waiting for others to do it.

Businesses are actively seeking out people like you. Never have employees of color had more opportunities to take up space than now. The world wants to hear from you. Working at a media conglomerate and being in the trenches of decision-making on conversations around promoting more inclusive and diverse voices on TV, I can tell you we *need* you and your voice. The tides are truly shifting, so use them in your favor.

Owning your playbook, your leadership style, will allow you to take your career to the next level. It's time to flip the script and play bigger. Instead of asking yourself, *Am I worthy of being here?*, you need to start asking yourself, *Are they worthy of having me?*

Never underestimate your struggle, grit, or resilience. The very root of it all is your own superpower for success.

12

The Power of the Other

If someone had told me that I eventually would go from Dreamer to TV producer, journalist, and author, I would have thought they were impossibly naive. Don't get me wrong—I was working hard to succeed in life. These were the roles and jobs I wanted, yet I struggled to say them out loud. At times they felt like they were too big for someone like me. Yet none of this stopped me from envisioning what success would look like for me.

Throughout the zigzag of opportunities and obstacles I've faced, I've realized that a big part of succeeding in our efforts is a certain level of entitlement. Yes, that icky word, entitlement! Entitlement means that you inherently believe you deserve something. This permission to feel like we deserve opportunities to thrive is a major ingredient that can help us get from a place of scarcity to a place of success. Before we can convince anyone to invest or believe in us, we have to do it for ourselves. We need to start believing that we have the capability of reaching those big aspirational jobs, roles, and occupations we want to be a part of.

No matter where you are in achieving your vision of success, you must continue to communicate about, write down, and plan for your goals, especially those that feel audacious and a little scary. Know with every fiber of your being that you can do that big thing or become that person you want to be.

And please don't feel apologetic about it. I wanted to highlight and bring more diverse voices to the tables that I was seated at. I didn't know *how* or through what medium this goal would take place or what experience would get me there. But these intentions were all sitting in my gut, and that was what got me through some of the most challenging times. Often I had to overlook my immigration status or some other cultural bias to focus on my vision. I had to trust in something greater, and I want you to do this too.

When you put your energy and intention toward what you want and what truly matters—your *why*—and you do your part, what you can control in the world will shift for you. The closed doors, gridlock, dead ends will open. As women of color, LGBTQ people, and all kinds of "others" in the workplace, we don't have white male privilege, but we still get creative and we win. We can become trailblazers and go beyond preestablished rules.

The first word that always comes to mind for our community is "resilience." Even when faced with uncertainty and a number of factors that are out of our control, there is an empowering truth to be found: *Nothing can stop us.* We control our narrative, and we have the ability to go beyond how our environment defines us—in ways that are creative, different, more colorful, fuller, because we have a bigger spectrum of understanding the human condition in all its juxtapositions and duality, simply by living in the world as ourselves.

My own great truth that I continue to embrace is that I don't belong—and I am grateful for that now. I've worked my butt off and have gone from being a behind-the-scenes booking producer to becoming a full-time MSNBC reporter. Instead of feeling out of my league, I now feel empowered by being exactly who I am.

Embracing our not-belonging breaks the chains of complicity with structural forces that do not serve us. As we learn to take up space and allow our multidimensionality to shine through, we are also breaking down that old framework and rebuilding it to create our own box.

I once asked Isabel Allende, the world-renowned Chilean author of many *New York Times* best-selling novels, who has lived in the United States for many years, if she had ever felt the struggle to choose one identity over another or felt like she didn't fully belong to either Chilean or American culture. She said, "I have always been a foreigner. I never felt like I totally belonged in one place, and I've never tried to assimilate to the point of leaving behind my culture, my language, the way I look. I think I can have everything. Why should I have less? I have more. It's good to be bicultural."

Why should we feel like we have to choose or trade our beautiful, layered identity for anything? We shouldn't—not for a place, a thing, a person, or a workplace. Our connection to the human condition—its contradictions, richness, complexity, diversity, and wholeness—is even clearer to us because of the crosscurrents of our identities. We have a better ability to understand the world and the people around us with more depth. That is power. Power we shouldn't give away.

You'll inevitably continue to have moments of uncertainty. You may still experience struggle, bias, and prejudice, still doubt yourself at times and wrestle with limiting beliefs. So keep the tools and practices that we've explored throughout this book in mind to help you navigate these moments and experiences.

Even though at the moment of writing this, I'm still in limbo—the almost 800,000 DACA recipients in this country still don't have a path to legalization. DACA was the door to opportunity, but my relentless hard work, sacrifice, discipline, and strategy is what got me to the other side of that opening.

I've had to live with multiple identities that have existed in different pockets of my life—being an immigrant, and a Latina, and a DACA recipient, and an American-raised foreigner no longer feels confusing or messy. It feels rich, empowering, deliciously authentic, and unique. I wouldn't trade it for the world. That's why I reject being cast aside. I reject limiting my own vision through the eyes of another person, and you should too.

Our identity is ours, and ours alone. Something of our own creation. Something only we can intimately know, that no one but us can define. In order to bulletproof our future, we've got to charge forward in our careers with confidence and power. Women of color, children of immigrants, the LGBTQ community, and any other type of marginalized community are making it happen through our own determination, hard work, and focus. So own it.

It's up to us to be kind to ourselves, set boundaries, give ourselves grace and space, say no to less, and reject self-judgment, guilt, and shame. On our way to the top, owning power and space in our work also means taking care of ourselves and our needs and practicing self-care.

We must also accept that we are worthy and have compassion for our journeys (and the journeys of others) in order to be effective, empathetic leaders. We have to extend that same love and kindness to others and to ourselves.

Remember that you deserve the most. If you've done everything in your power and still feel stuck or bogged down in an impossible toxic environment, if you've bent over backward time and again and have finally reached a boiling point because you honestly feel undervalued at work, maybe it's time for an exit plan. In addition to focusing on raises and promotions, it's also important to take inventory and come to terms with when it might be time for a bigger change.

Leaving a job that is no longer satisfying your *why* doesn't mean you've failed. On the contrary, change is difficult, but it fosters growth. Once you remove the blinders and open that new door, you may see opportunities you never even realized were already right there within your reach. Don't settle. Some companies are just not worthy of your talents and skills. Remember, with the right strategy, self-imposed ground rules, and perseverance, the uncertainty of handling your own expanding professional path can be manageable.

Your journey is necessary not just for you but also for those who will come after you. It is your way of moving up and the character you show that starts to create a precedent for the next generation. There's no use in silencing ourselves, because stepping into our power isn't just about us. Paving the path for those who come after us is also at stake. If we begin to see our individual trajectories as part of the seeds we leave behind for the next generation of women like us to plant, we can start to become emboldened by the power of our ascension.

As we move further up the ladder, we may have to embrace being different variations of "the only" at the top. Being the only Latina and one of only a few women in a male-dominated environment for many years, I get it. I've also heard many women talk about this feeling, especially when they get further ahead in their careers and are holding their own in leadership roles. As you transform into a more confident, outspoken, assertive, badass version of yourself, chances are you will still come across people who perceive you as harsh or too ambitious, and some may end up not liking you. That is the truth of our culture. There are some people who will never fully relinquish their biases around strong, confident women of color who break the mold of what is expected. But you can decide if you want that to be a lonely place or if you want to seek out a band of professional allies to navigate these spaces with more solidarity in order to push forward. And they don't necessarily have to be part of your own company.

That's what I had in mind when I created Acceso, a community of professional allies dedicated to access, opportunity, and mentorship. It's a place where women in their early-to-middle careers can find a safe space, live mentorship, and exclusive content to help them solve a specific career pain point. It provides a support system for and by women all around the world in these crucial years when it's key to lay the right foundation to advocate for ourselves now and in the future. Consider joining professional organizations that will provide empathy and support to help keep you uplifted in real life.

We must work, together and as individuals, to manage our careers and effectively define our own stories and intentions in a way that honors us. Our collective force has the power to break down barriers, structural inequalities, and self-limiting beliefs, giving way to a more equitable and fair playing field. And it starts with you. Let's step away from accommodating others, waiting for permission, and treading lightly, and instead assume the power that we already have. Feel that power in yourself. You are the new future of work—how will you leave your mark?

Own that voice inside of you. Be what you want to see, and charge forward. I'm here with you, doing the same, and cheering you on.

Acknowledgments

Thank you to my editorial team: Krishan, Amina, Cecilia, Kathryn, Abimael, and the rest of the team at Hachette, for believing in this message and seeing it through.

Johanna, I am so happy our paths crossed. I can't wait to see what comes next, from what I hope is the beginning of a long partnership. Mil gracias por creer en mi.

My family, friends, and OG members of Acceso Community, who have supported me through these last few years of this long writing process and read through these pages—thank you for your encouragement and support.

Mika, Joe, Willie, Alex, Rachel, Mike, Cat, Dan, Mike B, Rachael, Ann, Lorie, and the entire *Morning Joe* team, thank you for your support. I feel so lucky to be part of the best morning show team around and surrounded by the hardest-working and most talented people in the business.

Mika—for being a true sponsor, believing in me, and going to bat for me time and time again. We need more leaders and women like you. I am so endlessly grateful for your mentorship and the incredible opportunities you've placed in my path. I would not be here without you.

Dina y Raul—for always looking after me and giving me the love of reading and books.

My mom and my second mom, Mary—my best friends, cheerleaders, and support system. I wouldn't be who I am without you. Las quiero mucho.